BECOMING

A

CREATIVE

ENTREPRENEUR

Your GPS to Business Success

*A 50-Year Journey of One of Our
Most Creative Entrepreneurs*

JACK FECKER

*"I would have paid $1000 for this book when
starting my first business at age 27!"*

AVIVA
PUBLISHING
NEW YORK

BECOMING A *CREATIVE* ENTREPRENEUR
Your GPS to Business Success
A 50-Year Journey of One of Our Most Creative Entrepreneurs

CONTACT for Speaking Engagements/Media Interviews
Seminars/Consulting/Book Signings/Business Mentoring
J. Bakken
huntress4authors@comcast.net
425.333.5246

ISBN: 978-0-9841497-6-6
Library of Congress # 2009910152

Editor: Jane Bakken
Technical Editor: Tyler Tichelaar
Cover, Jacket, Interior Design: Fusion Creative Works

Every attempt has been made to source properly all quotes.
Seattle Times article printed with permission from Seattle Times
Printed in United States of America
First Edition
2 4 6 8
For Additional Copies, visit:
www.BecomingACreativeEntrepreneur.com

"As no stream can rise higher than its source,

So you can give no more or better to architecture than you are.

So why not go to work on yourselves and make yourselves

In quality what you would have your buildings be.

Frank Lloyd Wright
Addressing group of
Architectural students in 1950

Jack Fecker's Revision for Entrepreneurs

"As no stream can rise higher than its source,

So you can give no more or better to business than you are.

So why not go to work on yourselves and make yourselves

In quality what you would have your business be."

DEDICATION

To my wife, Jane

My Children ~
Lorrie, David and Jason

My Grandchildren ~
Brittany, Blayne, Jenna, Luke and Jonah

Acknowledgements

To all my family and friends ~ Your loving support throughout the whole of my life receives my deepest gratitude.

To all my business colleagues, partners, managers, investors, employees ~ The life lessons I have learned from each of you would fill a library.

Jane, my wife and editor ~ You never cease to amaze me. March, 1982, we began this soulful journey, and every day your huge love inspires me to be all I can be, as a man, partner, father, friend and as an entrepreneur. I could not have asked for a better soulmate, and I look forward to our next twenty-seven years together. Your editing, as always, is a work of art!

Lorrie, my daughter ~ Your endless creativity has always been an inspiration to me from the moment you were born. I'm trying to just keep up with you!

David, my son ~ You have taught me more than you can imagine. I am open and excited to continue learning from your wisdom. I am proud of all you have created in your life, and thrilled to watch your own "entrepreneur" creating profitable adventures in the marketplace.

Jason, my son ~ You have always attracted great people and adventures into your life, easily. I look forward to practicing in the marketplace, and every area of life, the knowledge and wisdom that you seem to be born with.

Patrick Snow ~ International Best-Selling Author of *Creating Your Own Destiny,* International Speaker, Publishing Coach and Internet Entrepreneur. Thank you for being such a phenomenal coach in writing and speaking. I owe you big time for your powerful contributions and excellent guidance in the publishing of this book. I look forward to our growing relationship in years to come!

Shiloh/Fusion Creative Works ~ Cover, Jacket and Interior Design and Layout. Your creativity and mastery of your craft has turned this book into a work of art. Thank you so much!

Tyler Tichelaar ~ technical editor. Thank you for your great skills and attention to detail. You were a critical part of making this book most excellent!

Bob Farrell ~Creator of Farrell's Ice Cream Parlours, International Author of *Give 'Em The Pickle,* and International Professional Speaker. You have always been a role model for me to stay focused on my goals. Your creations of Farrell's Ice Cream Parlour Restaurants set a standard giving the entrepreneur in me the opportunity to thrive. With your non-stop inspiration and ideas, you taught me continually to think big and always outside of the box. Thanks for giving me my first personal growth book ~ *Think and Grow Rich,* by Napoleon Hill. Without you, my business career would never would have been this much fun!

Joe Rutten ~ Friend since 1939, Business Partner for seventeen years in The Blue Banjo, Louie's Old Chicago, and Elroy's Ice Cream Parlour, Farrell's Ice Cream Parlour Restaurants (NW Territorial franchise) and Yonny Yonsons. Who knew when we were selling eggs and corn door-to-door as partners at age six that we would have end up creating so many years of such a great partnership! I learned more from you than any other business partner. Our on-going success hinged on your expertise in all those areas that I was not very strong. What a great time we've had. Thank you, my friend

Bill Keegan ~ Partner in Breadline & Soup Kitchen. Thank you for teaching me that good taste in food and all of life finds its source in my emotions. I'll never forget all the fun memories we had in creating this great establishment. Your strengths and energy were always a huge part of its success!

Al Fleenor ~ Management/Farrell's Ice Cream Parlours; Owner/President CEO (Retired) of Pacific Coast Restaurants, Inc. You were one of the greatest managers I ever worked with. It is no surprise that you became the most successful businessman of all our employees, eventually building some thirty formal dining restaurants in nine different brands. Your openness to new ideas and your teachable spirit set you apart from all others. I'll never forget your stellar dedication in driving four hours round trip every week from your Farrell's restaurant in Tri-Cities just to attend our management meetings in Seattle. I recall vividly how much employees enjoyed working for you and thriving under your management style. You were always the kind of manager I wanted to be!

John Boyle ~ Creator of the Omega Seminars, where I learned the value of 100% responsibility for my actions and the freedom that came with that knowledge.

Mark Victor Hansen ~ International Published Author, including *Chicken Soup for the Soul* series, International Professional Speaker/Consultant/Seminar Leader. Thank you for your connection and friendship. From you I learned to keep creating a very large "want list" and the FUN of receiving what I want instead of what I don't want.

Charlie Tremendous Jones ~ Published Author, Inspirational Speaker, and Seminar Leader. From the first time I met you in Seattle in the 70's, you inspired me always to be excited about my work, and whatever I was doing. As a result, every day I went to work with the anticipation of the best of possibilities, and have been passing on your contagious optimism to all those I've worked with in the marketplace ~ thank you, Charlie!

Ron Connor, Friend ~ You always ask the tough questions at the right time, and provide support and inspiration for me when I most need it. Thank you.

Sheila Connor, Friend and Business Colleague. Thank you for teaching me how to give wonderful seminars. You have taught me so much of how to bring out the best in individuals and businesses alike, and your friendship is always treasured.

Stan Day, Friend ~ Though you have had more challenges than anyone should have in three lifetimes, you have still been there for me through all these years…thank you, friend.

Rev. Max Lafser ~ Minister/Public Speaker/Seminar Leader and Friend (also officiated our wedding). When Jane and I are with you and Rama, we laugh continually, no matter what life and the marketplace is throwing at us! Thank you for encouraging me thirty-five years ago to get up on that stage and always to give my best!

Rama Vernon ~ Friend and Global Teacher/Diplomat. Your ability to imagine and work on a global level has always inspired me to reach for the highest in myself. In your presence, I am inspired to always reach for the most creative, the most fun, and the most innovative ideas.

Dr. Timothy Weber ~ Wise and Inspirational Coach. You have always had the more powerful answers to my questions. Thank you for gifting me with the "integrity" definition for which I had been hunting (see Chapter 3).

Nancy Nordgren - Gifted Counselor. Thank you for the many years of your care and support in traveling more into my body with mind and spirit. It has been well worth the journey!

CONTENTS

FOREWORD

BY BOB FARRELL

Creator of Farrell's Ice Cream Parlour Restaurants, International Professional Speaker and International Author of *Give 'Em The Pickle*

Jack Fecker and I first met when the original Farrell's Ice Cream Parlour Restaurant was under construction. Even then, before we ever connected on a business level, Jack was a great encouragement to me in those initial strenuous and doubtful days when I was first opening a new business. From the early days of the original conception of the business, Jack Fecker provided a great deal of the pizzazz, promotional ideas and art work used in our 145 Farrell's restaurants throughout the States. In my opinion, Jack has an astounding ability to come up with an awful lot of original ideas concerning restaurants, or any business. He is certainly one of the best concept idea men I have ever met!

Through the years, I've observed that Jack Fecker possesses one ability missing from so many creative people in business. He always had the strength to communicate his ideas to others ~ managers and employees ~ in such a way that they were able to make the ideas a reality, faster and more easily.

Many of our concepts at Farrell's carried on through the years evolved out of our first few years of business, and Jack was involved in most of our "idea sessions" during that time. Jack eventually went out on his own and has proven himself over and over again as an exceptional creative entrepreneur and successful businessman.

I cannot speak highly enough of Jack Fecker. I know that he has been and will continue to be a tremendous mentor to entrepreneurs and companies everywhere. Jack's insights into creativity, brainstorming, and all the building blocks required in developing a new business, and in revitalizing and expanding a struggling business, will increase the profitability for many companies.

In October 2009, we are excited about our Farrell's Ice Cream Parlours beginning their second lifetime with the first stores being built in Los Angeles. When the call was made for new employees, more than 800 showed up. I have no doubt that parents with memories of our FUN restaurants are encouraging their sons and daughters to show up for this opportunity. Without a doubt, Jack Fecker played a significant role in developing the reputation of excellence in our Farrell's Ice Cream Parlours that is now being handed down to a new generation.

If entrepreneurs start new businesses for the purpose of serving their customers in a manner superior to that being done anywhere else, they will have a job for life!

Jack Fecker has lived this motto as an entrepreneur throughout the whole of his life with great continuity and dedication.

This book is an exceptional gift to all business professionals and entrepreneurs. In these pages, there is a wisdom that Jack has been gleaning over more than five decades. I have no doubt that his ability to share this wisdom with humor, anecdotes and pragmatic action steps will go on to encourage and inspire that band of entrepreneurial adventurers and explorers of business for many generations to come!

Becoming A Creative Entrepreneur ~ Your GPS to Business Success is an excellent book! Anyone running a business or wanting to start a new business should absolutely read this book!

Bob Farrell

Bob Farrell,
Creator of Farrell's Ice Cream Parlour Restaurants
International Professional Speaker
International Author of the book, *Give 'Em The Pickle*
www.GiveEmThePickle.com
Watch for Farrell Ice Cream Parlour Restaurants coming once again to your city! Initial opening in LA, Oct., 2009

INTRODUCTION

As this book is heading into its first printing in 2009, we find ourselves at a time in our economic history when we have never needed creative entrepreneurs more. Becoming a creative entrepreneur will be significant in the business of the future. Integrating linear and creative structures and systems will be the norm at every level of the business model and at the center of its DNA. Building on the foundational blocks of the agricultural, industrial and informational ages, we are moving into a conceptual age that will ask of all business owners in the marketplace a level of ingenuity and of creative thinking that we are just now beginning to explore more fully in this Twenty-First Century.

I sincerely believe in the public sector. I also believe passionately in the power of visionaries, adventurers and explorers infused with an entrepreneurial spirit. I believe wholeheartedly that we as creative entrepreneurs will be the leaders in the marketplace who pragmatically map out new possibilities dictated by supply and demand that will not only bolster our national economy, but will address in a more effective manner the business of global needs ‚ innovative energy solutions and the "greening" of our planet, world hunger, healthcare, education and affordable housing, to name a few.

For more than fifty years, I have been on this adventure of becoming a "creative entrepreneur," and in my estimation, there has never been a better time for me to pass on some of the details, knowledge and wisdom gleaned over these past five decades.

The tools and ideas passed on to you in these pages have been market-tested tough during my startup of more than twenty businesses. They have stood the test of time in facilitating hundreds of entrepreneurs and business professionals in beginning their own ventures, as well as in the development and profitable selling of companies by entrepreneurs.

Along the way, I have made many powerful discoveries, some more powerful than others. One of the most valuable thoughts I've used is that there is no right or wrong way to accomplish anything. Over the years, I discovered a powerful phrase in describing how I do things, which is "something is more or less powerful." This is a statement generating questions that can serve to flush out your next steps in any venture. Is there a more powerful way to approach this project? If you were to do this over again, what things might you do differently? Could you perhaps try a new way? Is there something we have not thought of yet?

Let's try using the word "maybe," another word that is not quite so loaded.

"Maybe" we could take a little time and think this over. "Maybe" these action steps will be beneficial, "maybe" not. I've discovered that in approaching any concept in business with phrases such as "maybe," "perhaps," "less powerful and more powerful," that a great deal more can be accomplished. In my professional opinion, much less is accomplished using phrases such as right, wrong, good, bad, better or best, all of which will stifle the creative process.

I would have gladly invested $1,000 to have the tools outlined in this book at the age of twenty-seven when I started my first business. It would have saved me considerable time, money and energy, more than you can possibly imagine. I am confident that the manner in which these tools are presented in this book will enable you, today's entrepreneur, to benefit tremendously from my own successes, failures, experiments and discoveries.

I have always seen myself as my own guinea pig - experimenting, trying this idea, making mistakes, coming up with a new way and starting all over again when something didn't quite work out as planned. One thing I know about myself is that in the arena of business and in matters of the marketplace, I am persistent and possess a high degree of patience. The importance of these two characteristics will be discussed fully throughout my marketplace stories.

This book is set up in three sections:

SECTION I: HOW DO I CREATE MY OWN BUSINESS…

USING A PRIORITY, STEP-BY-STEP PROCESS LEADING UP TO THE OPENING DAY. STARTING WITH YOUR OPENING IDEA, NOW WHERE DO YOU GO FROM HERE?

This Section includes:

- Identifying the "IDEA"

- Creating well-defined, long-range impossible goals; discovering how these will serve you

- Bringing your vision to life

- Integrating your own personal Core Values into the foundation of your business

- Mining the hidden secrets of treasure mapping in bringing your goal into reality

- Steps in using creative storyboards to save time in organizing your creation

- Creating structural tension and making it work <u>for</u> vs. against you

- Putting enthusiasm to work for you ~ getting excited about your work

- How to put your business idea in picture form utilizing theater set designs

- The game of brainstorming; Idea-Generation: How to create 100 ideas per hour when you want a solution that is easy, with the least amount of effort and cost

- Value of finding and secrets of maintaining a profitable business partnership

SECTION II: OPEN FOR BUSINESS...NOW WHAT DO I DO?

<u>This Section includes:</u>

- The importance and un-importance of start-up capital

- Putting the "Ten Unique Factors" to work

- Ten steps for operating a powerful, exciting, profitable and FUN business

- Discovering and using all your strengths

- Finding those great employees for your specific business

- Making delegation an easy part of your daily routine

- Learning how to become more creative

- Alignment ~ Creating it, and how it differs from "agreement"

SECTION III: HOW TO NURTURE YOURSELF WHILE GROWING YOUR BUSINESS

This Section includes:

- Learning to value mis-takes

- Starting your own vision circle support group (detailed guidelines)

- Planning your 100th Birthday Party with guest list and life contributions

- Integrating the value of "spirit" for profitable business practices

- Nurturing yourself in every area of life while growing your business

- Asking for help

- Letting go of control

- Letting go of procrastination by using the "do it now" principle

- Scheduling time for "play"

- And most important! A daily "gratitude exercise"

I am certain you will enjoy trying and using these ideas as much as I have.

Remember ~ all the FUN is in the journey!

SECTION ONE

HOW DO I CREATE MY OWN BUSINESS?

Steps Leading up to Opening Day

CHAPTER 1

IDEA

Why do we always begin with an idea? Because it is the most essential nugget of any project, plan, design, goal or any business. It is the kernel from which everything else tangible springs to life. Imagination plays a primary role in the idea process for it is the soil in which all ideas are fed and nurtured, eventually sprouting and making their way to the surface of outer reality.

People with fertile imaginations are those individuals rich with an abundance of ideas. And ideas are a close sibling to choices, an imperative in solving problems. You will find that excellent problem solvers are idea-people rich with vibrant imaginations.

Solutions to any problem are waiting around every corner. We only need to be open to receiving. And there it is! A faster way to accomplish something, an easier method to perform a task, a more powerful way to attract customers, a new product or service needed in the marketplace, and each originating with the seed of an idea.

Everything begins with an idea. Webster's Dictionary defines "idea" like this: "Something one thinks, knows or imagines; a thought; mental conception or image; notion."

And every idea began with a thought in someone's mind. What we too often forget is every detail of our daily lives has its origin in a simple thought. From homes, cars, windows and pavement to your silverware and plates on the table, even the table, their origin grew from one single thought.

Everything that appears had its origin in the mind. Our minds evolve the ideas, and nurtured through the imagination and our memories of senses, they begin to express themselves through words and pictures.

In 1957, I was twenty-five years old and made frequent trips between Seattle and San Francisco, my favorite place to visit. I would often visit The Red Garter in the Broadway District where they served beer and peanuts with a five-piece banjo band playing all the old sing-along tunes. It was the most exciting nightclub in the Bay Area, and most nights of the week, you were lucky if you could get a seat. Just seeing that place fired up my imagination until it was working overtime. I had a hunch this was a concept that was needed in the marketplace, and it would be well received in my hometown of Seattle.

At the time, I was a Boeing engineer with a secure job. Within three years, I was leading my own banjo band in an old-fashioned 1890's bar in downtown Seattle, and soon, it became the most popular nightclub spot in the Northwest. It was called The Blue Banjo, with seating for 300 customers, and we always boasted of at least 100 people standing in line waiting to get in on weekends!

The point I'm making is whenever you experience something that has powerful energy for your body, mind and spirit, pay attention, for this is often the origin of a "big idea."

The vision or picture I held in my mind was "a very popular night club with lots of folks having a good time with me playing in the band and people standing in line to get in."

In 1936, **Charles Fillmore** stated in his book, ***Prosperity,*** *"The idea is the most important factor in every act and must be given first place in our attention if we would bring about any results of a permanent character."*

If one idea were so important, why wouldn't more, a lot more, be even more valuable? I don't believe one can have too many ideas on any one project. That is why I developed a method for generating 100 ideas an hour on any one question or problem. Let me put it this way. If you were going to hire someone to work for you or with you, wouldn't you rather select from 100 individuals instead of only three or four? Well, it's the same with ideas. Having more choices will only give you a better chance of creating the results you want.

Ideas come to me every day. I practice paying attention to the ones that are exciting and generate the most energy. For those of you who say, "I never have any good ideas," I offer this suggestion: never say that statement again! Instead, replace it with this thought and statement, "I am open to all the ideas and choices that come into my mind." In 1973, I wrote these words: "I am accomplishing my life goals by soaking up ideas and learning like a sponge."

You see, it all starts with one of my favorite things to do which is "idea-generation." At times, it is referred to as "brainstorming" where you gather others to join in idea-generation, which will be covered in detail in Chapter 8. Someone once told me, "Ideas are like slippery fish." You can hang onto them but for a brief moment. That's why "idea people" always carry a note pad or cards with them at all times. Nowadays, an i-pod or computer notebook might come in handy. You generally have only two or three seconds to write an idea down before it flits away and gets lost by some distraction.

You've probably heard the story of how the Harry Potter books and movies all began their life. The creator, J.K. Rowling, was in a train rumbling across the countryside, and literally began this multi-million dollar concept by jotting down some simple ideas on a napkin. She seized the moment...having no "idea" where the train of those notes would take her! As a result, millions have enjoyed the books and movies that once were only a few scribbled ideas on a paper napkin.

A few years ago, someone reminded me, "A new idea is like making love to an elephant. If you're successful, it takes two years. If not, you'll be trampled to death." Another phrase I have heard many times was "Ideas are a dime a dozen." The fact of the matter is that many ideas can become worth many more dimes than you can carry when acted upon and put to good use.

I honestly believe I was attracted to the businesses I started because I could always see these ideas, through the kaleidoscope of my imagination, of how I could create something in a more efficient, faster, or more FUN manner than was being done in the marketplace at the present time. I have always been confident that I could generate the ideas to make something work in a more powerful way. If you believe that you have a "good idea," by all means, begin to act upon it, even if it is just writing it down on a paper napkin in a fast-moving train! This is what the following chapter is about

~ *Let's build a vision!*

CHAPTER 2

BUILDING A VISION

By the year 1963, my partners and I had created a nightclub called Louie's Old Chicago, next to The Blue Banjo, and also an ice cream parlor restaurant named Elroy's right across the street in the Old Pioneer Square section of Seattle. The origin of all these establishments was from our idea sessions we held on a weekly basis.

I was sitting having lunch at Elroy's one afternoon when in walked a man from Portland, Oregon. His name was Bob Farrell. Little did I know that this incredible idea man would one day be the recipient of the Horatio Alger Award for his ingenious creation and promotion of Farrell's Ice Cream Parlour Restaurants. This was a restaurant chain that would eventually number 136 stores, attracting overflow crowds in most major cities across America.

We sat and talked that first day when we met for almost three hours. From everything Bob Farrell told me, I felt his idea was a sound one. He said we should consider opening a Farrell's in Seattle after he and his partner opened one in Portland. At the time, I did not have a very clear idea of just how this new idea would work, or even what it would look like.

I told Bob I was going to New York to visit some relatives very soon, and he suggested that while I was there, I visit one of the more popular establishments, Jahn's Ice Cream Parlours. After all, he had worked in one of them when he was growing up. "It's similar to what I'm building in Portland," he explained. I felt I needed to get a picture of what he was talking about, so in a few months, I was sitting across the table talking to Frank Jahn, the owner of Jahn's Ice Cream Parlours in New York City. He told me at the time that his father had begun the ice cream business some seventy years back, and that he was now the second-generation owner.

Looking back, I realized that visiting Jahn's Ice Cream Parlours, and sitting in his creations, was vital as I began to build a vision of this idea of Farrell's Ice Cream Parlours. My partner, Joe Rutten, and I were already mulling over the idea of opening a number of ice cream parlors in the area. Our preliminary research was clear that we could create more income from selling ice cream than beer. The beer business was limited to mostly after hours, and ice cream was a fourteen-hour/day business, a "cold, hard" fact that was proven in the months and years to come in selling 1000's of gallons of ice cream.

There were other trips to LA and San Francisco so I could continue to see firsthand exactly what types of ice cream stores were flourishing. After several discussions with Bob Farrell and completing all of my research visits, I felt strongly that we were definitely on the right track. As a result, I told my partner that we should definitely consider the offer proposed to us by Bob Farrell for this new venture.

I learned a valuable lesson in meeting with individuals who were involved already with something I thought I would enjoy, and I was always asking a couple of key questions. When I met with the owner of Jahn's in New York, I was sure to ask how he had started the stores, and what two things would he have done differently if he were to begin all over again?

After the history lesson, which was always a valuable ice breaker, Jahn confessed that the two things he would have done differently were 1) make sure he had enough land for a sixty-car parking lot, and 2) farm out the manufacturing of the ice cream. Not allowing for these two items from the beginning of his business had ended up hurting his profits through the years.

As a result, my partner and I added to our "idea picture" for our new ice cream franchises lots of parking, and no manufacturing hassles.

Bob Farrell opened his first dream ice cream restaurant in Portland on Twenty-First and Burnside to rave reviews. With this prototype and a commitment from Farrell to partner with us, Joe and I eagerly set out to find the ideal location. However, we had no idea at the time that it would take a full year to find a landlord who would even consider signing a lease with us. Our vision intact, even after numerous turndowns, we were finally successful in securing a landlord in Bellevue, Washington, across the lake from Seattle, just across the street from Nordstrom's which was ideal. And the best part was that it came with a parking lot for at least sixty cars!

It's important to note that while we were hunting for the ideal location, we had no more than $2,000 coming to us from the projected sale of our nightclub, and we knew that it was going to take a minimum investment of $5,000 for our half of the bargain. We managed to borrow $1,000 from a friend with a promissory note to pay back in one year. What confidence we must have had! And we did have that most valuable of all ingredients ~ a healthy, vivid vision!

It was now time to take that leap that only entrepreneurs seem to have embedded in their DNA. We sold our remaining interest in The Blue Banjo to two individuals from whom we received our $2,000 each to move ahead. Farrell and his partner put in $5,000, and the dairy co-signed the note to the bank for the equipment and fixtures.

There was no going back now, so we were fiercely committed to doing whatever it took to succeed. We each worked an average of 100 hours per week for the first three or four months, and took very little salary as we had thirty-six employees to train and pay weekly.

This chapter's main point is to give you an example of the tools used to create a clear picture of what you want. We had to build a clear picture of what it would look like to run a successful business operation, and that is the vision we clung to, through thick and thin. My imaginary movie in building eating establishments always included long waiting lines of customers. That can also translate into more orders than you can fill. Partners would sometimes ask me, "What if too many people show up?" My stock answer always was, "Don't Worry! We'll figure it out."

When you are creating your own vision, always see it big and keep it simple. I believe most of us don't go for the big goal, the big picture, the large vision. Think outside of the box, outside of your comfort zone. When you have that impossible dream, hold on to it! Write it down, picture it, feel it, smell it, hear it, touch it. Trust that whatever you can hold in your mind, even if it is for only a few seconds in the beginning, you can create. That is how big ideas are brought into reality. Whenever I want to create something new, I need to get out of the way and let my <u>subconscious and the power of my imagination</u> bring in the horsepower to do the work.

Visions, pictures and imaging ~ these are the building blocks of the foundation upon which all business ventures stand. Without them, the structure will be too weak to survive. As you progress and begin to take the action steps to make the vision a reality, it is also extremely valuable to have others holding the vision with you. It is as if they are "praying" for your success in this action. Great visionaries are able to articulate their ideas via word pictures, conveying the life of a vision to others, until everyone around them is holding the same vision with them. Great leaders are those who know how to do this with millions of people.

Here are a few to prime the pump:

- An automobile so cheap that every person can afford one.

- A man walking on the moon.

- A PC on every person's desk.

- A wireless cell phone in the hands of every individual.

These are all visions that were placed before us by great visionaries until they came true. And whether a leader inspires others to implement a path of destruction, or of new beginnings, the potency comes back to this one thing: they had the ability to convey the life of that vision to millions of people in such a way that it's spark caught fire and created results.

Imagine what we could create in the world, in the marketplace, in our homes, our families, our communities, if we could pass this one truth on to every young person: That it all begins with an idea, a thought, a vision, and that individuals do have the power to create their reality. "Heroes" featured on CNN as well as the Teacher of the Year Awards by Walt Disney are two examples illustrating how we might spread this powerful propaganda in practical and entertaining ways.

Every single person on the planet has the ability to do this. And while I do believe that entrepreneurs have an edge, I also believe, that with a little practice, and starting with small things and working up to the biggies, any individual can master the art of visioning and creating, even if you're not an entrepreneur.

On one of our many road excursions to Portland, Oregon, Bob Farrell handed me a valuable little book, *Think and Grow Rich*, by Napoleon Hill. After reading it, I learned the value of writing down my goals. My partner and I initially wrote down six goals we wanted to reach in ten years. We jotted them down on 3x5 cards we each carried in our billfolds. Every so often, we would take out our cards and read them. The amazing thing was that we reached all six goals in less than six years.

Since that time, I have been writing down, frequently, short and long-range goals. Written goals are a major part of building a vision. I've often wondered why more people don't try this. There is abundant evidence that suggestions made to our subconscious through our senses…visual, hearing, writing, etc. are powerful stimuli, and it costs little or nothing to do. And if you fail, it's really not that big of a deal because you just start over. That is, unless, of course, you are afraid. What's the worst thing that can happen? Well, that you don't reach your goal, but you did reach other goals along the way that you would not have had without that one destination in your mind. Every year when I write down my ten goals, while I'm doing it, I also make it okay not to reach any of them. I also make a point to celebrate when any one of them is attained.

These written goals are an important part of the visioning process. Create a physical picture of your idea whatever it is…a product, a store, a building, a new job, a fulfilling relationship…anything. In 1973, after weekly idea sessions for six months on a restaurant concept, I found the perfect way for it to become a visual picture that would be so loaded with energy for all of us involved that the subsequent action steps came easy.

I decided to make a trip to the local repertory theater to find out how the staff members there designed their sets. The person I spoke with explained how each production would originate with a set designer who created colorful sketches of the stage set they wanted to build. It just so happened that their current designer was visiting from New York where he was renowned for creating some of the finest opera and Broadway show sets in the Big Apple.

As fortune had it, I was introduced and met with John Wright Stevens from Manhattan that same day, and upon my request and offer of compensation, he agreed to produce five watercolor drawings of our new restaurant concept, each 20x24 inches in size. These drawings not only helped convince skeptics to support our venture, but they were the main reason we were able to enlist the support of bankers, securing a substantial bank loan. They say a picture is worth a thousand words. Well, in this case, five pictures were worth five thousand words! In short, the restaurant was built, and the bulk of the ideas in the sketches became a living reality.

Sometimes you need all the help you can get with your visioning process.

In review, remember these steps:

1. Find out if anyone is doing what you want to do. Seek them out and ask what they would do differently if they were to start over.

2. Create ideas on how you can make it better.

3. Write down 5–10 goals you want to accomplish. If you are in partnership with someone, make sure your partner is in total alignment with those goals.

4. Do everything possible to connect your idea with picture form. Sketch it out, or have someone else do it

for you. Write down word pictures to begin with. Take a photograph of something similar, or cut pictures from magazines.

In Chapter 4, we will be exploring more of how we can create our own pictures of what we want to build in our lives.

CHAPTER 3

Core Values In Business

It was the middle of January, 1960, when Jack, owner of Jazz & Jack's Night Club, two blocks down from us, walked through the door at 7:05 p.m. It was a blustery, cold winter's Wednesday night, and we were setting up for another evening of fun at the Blue Banjo Night Club in the old Skid Road section of Seattle called Pioneer Square.

Six months earlier, I had purchased this old, run-down tavern with the $3,500 I had saved up from working as an engineer at Boeing. We still owed a balance of $6,500, and we were just getting by making payments, rent and funding a five-piece band. My salary at Boeing was $800 a month, and I took a $700/month pay reduction to make ends meet.

On this particular night, before any customers or band members had arrived, I was soon to stand face-to-face with fear, gut-wrenching fear. It was just before my twenty-eighth birthday, and I was definitely not prepared for what was about to happen.

Jack began explaining to me, in a matter-of-fact tone, that if I wanted my business to survive, I needed to start making payments to the police as well as to the liquor inspector.

"Do you mean to say that all these taverns and night club owners are involved in payoffs to the police?" I inquired.

"Yes," Jack responded. "And your first payment of $200.00 is due right now."

"Why should we all be paying and you get off scot-free without contributing?" he asked, in response to my explaining to him that we could not, and would not, go along with this.

Then came the hook intended to scare me into compliance.

"Last Saturday evening, your bartender, Jerry, served a woman under the age of twenty-one. In ten minutes from now, she will be entering your establishment with a police officer and will point out the individual who served her a beer."

He didn't need to go into further detail because I knew that if this occurred, we would be closed for one long week.

And if it happened a second time, we would lose our license and be closed for good.

Down deep I knew that this did not match up with my values, my values in life, or how I wanted to operate my business. Jerry pointed out that once we started paying, it would never end. So with all the nerve I could muster, I said, "No."

Sure enough, within ten minutes, in walked a policeman with a nineteen-year old who looked much older. Interestingly enough, she backed down and did not point out my bartender, and we did not get the citation that would have closed our doors to the public.

Although this was only the first of many future similar threats, saying "No" at this critical start-up point of our career made it much easier to follow suit in scenarios down the line.

We will all be tested in business at some point, and if integrity is not a core value at the top of your list, I assure you, it will be at the top of your list of reasons for your business failure. I didn't think about the ramifications much at the time since I was so young. But in hindsight, the core value of integrity has served me well over these past five decades in business, and more often than I can count.

Before you ever go into business, it is important to identify your basic values. We have seminars now that refer to them as "Core Values." These are the values that will guide you through difficult decisions usually arriving unannounced when they are least expected.

Let's take a closer look at this value of "Integrity." I believe Integrity is the most powerful core value one can have in his or her life, personal and professional. While I often define integrity simply as saying what you mean, and meaning what you say, Dr. Timothy Weber has a definition of integrity that I would like to share:

Integrity (Dr. Timothy Weber's definition reprinted with permission by him.)

Integrity = Wholeness. These are the five aspects of "wholeness."

A fair balance of give and take between a defined self who is attuned to the other so that there is a fair exchange of give and take, rights and obligations.

One who is a learning self, open to new possibilities and information…confident, not certain.

Honesty – speaking the truth and seeking the truth.

Creativity – using our whole self, our best gifts in new and creative ways.

Contribution – giving our gifts in service to the greater good.

What happened to all the dishonest owners and crooked police officers and liquor inspectors? Well, most of those businesses failed, and our new young governor, Dan Evans, dismissed the dishonest liquor inspectors. Within ten years, (yes, it took ten years!), the Seattle Police Department indicted and fired as many as fifty police officers for taking bribes and stealing.

During this time, I read a front-page article in the *Seattle Post Intelligencer* stating that there were absolutely no payoffs to the police in Seattle. I was so incensed by this that I remember going to a pay phone near the city railway station, dialing the *Seattle Times*, the other major newspaper, and talking with John Wilson, an investigative reporter, and his brother, Marshall. My warrior anger overcame any fears of being intimidated by the local police and what followed was the full front-page article reprinted by permission from the *Seattle Times*.

The Seattle Times

Weather Bureau forecast: Cloudy with chance of a few light showers. High in mid-40's; low tonight about 35. Southeast winds, 10 to 20. Chance of rain, 50%, tonight, 40%, tomorrow. High yesterday, 53; low overnight, 44. (Complete report, Page 34. Pass, ski report, Page 16.)

6 SECTIONS,   72 PAGES   SEATTLE, WASHINGTON, WEDNESDAY, JANUARY 25, 1967   PRICE TEN CENTS   ●

LIQUOR INSPECTOR ALSO MADE PAYOFF MOVES

Blue Banjo Ex-Owners Tell Of Harassment by Police

By JOHN WILSON and MARSHALL WILSON

Cigars, wrapped in $20 bills, once were suggested as the "key to successful living" in Seattle's police-payoff system, two former owners of the Blue Banjo, 610 First Av., have told The Times.

Jack Fecker, 35, and Joe Rutten, 32, who now operate Farrell's, an ice-cream parlor in Bellevue, said they are willing to testify before a committee named by Mayor Braman last week to probe reports of police payoffs published by The Times.

Their account is typical of reports obtained by The Times from dozens of sources in recent months.

The two said they will tell how they, for the most part, resisted demands for payoffs and subsequent harassments.

THE MEN, WHO BUILT UP the Blue Banjo from an "old run-down wine place" in 1959 to one of Seattle's leading night spots and a tourist attraction, left the night club about a year ago to open the Bellevue ice-cream parlor, which specializes in catering to birthday parties for children.

Fecker and Rutten credit the "respectability" of the Blue Banjo and "friends in high places" with allowing them to escape the payoff system.

The Blue Banjo has been used in promotional brochures as one of the city's leading tourist attractions. Members of the City Council frequently patronize the establishment.

"What would have happened if the business had been less respected but still a legal operation?" the two were asked.

"We wouldn't have lasted six months," Fecker said. "We would either have gone out of business or would have paid off to the police. If you don't have connections, there's no sense going into business—that kind of business, anyway."

Fecker said that in his first year of operation he was asked by a policemen to contribute a "case of liquor" for what he was told would be a City Council party.

Fecker said he "split the cost" of the case of liquor with the operator of another establishment, which also had been asked to supply a case, and police accepted the joint contribution.

"I later learned there was no City Council party," Fecker said.

WHEN THE BLUE BANJO first opened in 1959,

54

"right away a tavern operator came by and told me I was supposed to start paying off," Fecker said. Fecker refused, he said, because he was told by a friend "not to get started."

But Fecker said that shortly afterward the man who originally suggested he should pay the police came in one night and warned him that an under-age girl had been served in the Blue Banjo.

"He said that in about five minutes a state liquor inspector would come in, but I could avoid trouble if I would pay \$200," Fecker said.

"Sure enough, in about five minutes in came a liquor inspector, a Seattle policeman and a girl about 19. But the girl 'chickened out' and wouldn't put the finger on me."

On one occasion, the men said, a policeman suggested that "one way to avoid trouble is to wrap a cigar in a \$20 bill and stick it in the pocket of the liquor inspector whenever he came around."

Rutten said that one of the funny things about the payoff system was that "everyone was always asking for something for somebody else."

"Police were always telling us to take care of the liquor inspector," Rutten said. "The liquor inspector was telling us to take care of the police. And the other operator who told us of the payoff system was telling us to 'take care of everybody'."

"ANOTHER THING WE HAD TO DO was keep a bottle of whiskey in the back room," Fecker said. "This we did, because we didn't think it was payoff. It was supposed to be for the liquor inspector, but the cops used it, too."

The operators said that on one occasion a liquor inspector arrived at their establishment "so drunk" that he asked them:

"Where am I?"

Fecker and Rutten told about what they termed "police harrassment" after they refused to pay off.

"We had a young crowd—a lot different than most First Avenue places," Rutten said. "Policemen used to harass us by walking through the aisles, but the crowd wasn't doing anything wrong and they would 'boo' the police, as if they were part of the act. Police would get embarrassed and would leave!"

"We had one liquor inspector who was really a 'great guy'. He was new. He said that in a lot of places

he got $50 bills shoved at him and he would refuse. The money would be doubled, and he was offered $100."

"We told him that we thought 50 per cent of the taverns in town were paying off, but he told us we were wrong—he said it was closer to 95 per cent," Rutten said.

"When he came in we were shocked—here was a guy who finally treated us like businessmen."

The two said they talked, on numerous occasions, with various city officials, most of whom acknowledged that the situation was as they painted it, but nothing was done.

ON ONE OCCASION, the two said, they complained to a city councilman about the harassment and they said the councilman later told them he had advised police:

"Lay off the Blue Banjo, or we'll close up Chinatown!"

"I felt like we had the cleanest place in town," Fecker said, "but the police made us feel like we had the dirtiest place."

Another way they avoided the payoff system, the two said, was to "play dumb," pretending not to understand that demands were being made for a payoff.

"We just played dumb," they said. "We didn't try to fight them. The best thing is to play dumb."

Once, Fecker said, he found a policeman he had never seen before, sitting in the Blue Banjo office with a woman on his lap.

"The guy told me to bring two beers in the office. I brought them. I wasn't going to fight him," Fecker said. "I never saw the officer before and I've never seen him since."

Fecker and Rutten said that on numerous occasions they watched policemen, sometimes with women, entering and leaving a nearby tavern. They said the officers had a key to the place.

THE TWO SAID THEIR HARASSMENT continued, off and on, until they severed their connections with the Blue Banjo about a year ago.

"If we didn't like Seattle we wouldn't be talking about this," Fecker said. "But we think Seattle can be a good place to live."

Information Sought

The mayor's committee has asked that persons having information concerning police payoffs or misconduct write to Box 345, Main Postoffice.

Here are some of the most creative schemes we employed along the way.

One was when the head of the Vice Squad called my partner and me outside on the street to talk with us. He explained how we would be making payoffs. Being straight-arrow young men, we kept inquiring repeatedly, "How exactly do we do this? Where does this fit in our accounting records? What column would that be entered in?"

The guy became so frustrated when we told him we didn't have a clue how to make an illegal payment, and he blurted out, "Just take the money out of the till, wrap it around a cigar and put it in the lapel pocket of the liquor inspector." They were careful never to ask for themselves, but had set-up guys down the line who worked in cahoots with the others.

My partner, Joe, the accountant of our business, would ask, "Exactly how are we going to account for that money? We would have to report it on our tax statements." The guy would finally throw up his hands in frustration and walk away in disgust.

Another creative scheme I used was to place a small light fixture inside our upright piano and when the police or liquor inspector came down the street, our doorman would press a button that rang a bell installed behind the bar. The bartender would then flip a switch to turn on the light in the piano. At that exact moment, we would stop playing our instruments and dive into another song, one that customers would not be able to sing with, such as "Tiger Rag."

You see, one of the things they could harass us for was encouraging our patrons to participate in sing-a-longs. Under the law, during World War II, a cabaret license was required if you had any dancing or entertainment included as part of your establishment's business. This law required us as owners to pay 10% of everything we took in. The law was still in effect in 1960 and was repealed in 1965. It was considered entertainment if you encouraged a sing-a-long, but not if the band just played background music.

Although this was a federal law, the local police were using this to make our lives uncomfortable hoping we would give in. We had to pull this trick at least once every night on the weekends.

On other nights, a police officer would come by when the place was filled to capacity and tell us we were breaking the fire codes. I went to see the City Fire Chief who informed me that these guys were just hitting on us for payoffs. So the next time it happened, I just told the policeman to leave because he had no jurisdiction over the City Fire Department, and he left.

My point here is that when you are in business, it pays to stay calm, and stay one step ahead of anyone attempting to distract your focus from your clients.

If you spend most of your time and energy fighting the authorities and bureaucrats, your customers will suffer, along with you and your business.

There will be times in your future when the most important word in your vocabulary will be "No!" Use it wisely and with confidence in being true to your own core values, your integrity, and it will surely pay off in the long run.

CHAPTER 4

TREASURE MAPPING

Whatever you want to be, do or have can be made into a "treasure map." In the early 1980's, I was asked to demonstrate treasure mapping on the two major television stations in Seattle, Washington.

Treasure maps are like billboards advertising subliminal messages to your sub-conscious mind. They serve to entice you to buy whatever you are interested in selling yourself. In short, billboards work! If they didn't, major companies would not bother investing hundreds of thousands of dollars just for this purpose!

What I am suggesting is that a "treasure map" is the opportunity to build your own "billboard" for anything you wish to create in your life.

A simple way to get started:

- Take a colorful poster board (choose a color that gives you energy).

- Visualize a picture of what it is you desire.

- I choose a spiritual symbol and place this in the center of the board. This can be something you've found from a magazine or book; any symbol that centers you.

- Find a picture that is most similar to what it is you want ~ car, house, business, vacation spot, new appliance, or a great relationship. Paste the picture on one of the corners.

- Find some play money—Monopoly money is great!—totaling the amount you estimate it will take for the purchase, and paste this in one of the other corners. Write the amount in large numbers over the play money, and put *"This or better."* This step is not really necessary; however, it does seem to make it more fun.

- In one of the other corners, put in big letters **"FWP"** which stands for **"Fastest Way Possible."** This seems to work better than putting a specific date because you are now opening yourself up for the easiest, fastest way possible.

- On the remaining corner, I would suggest writing the word **"FUN"** or whatever words connect with you that describe the emotional feeling, pleasure or fun it will be to accomplish this dream.

The above process is essentially what I demonstrated on local television. After one of these shows, I had a lady call me and ask, "What goes on the bottom right-hand corner?" I responded with, "It doesn't really matter…in fact, none of this matters." She was surprised, but eventually got the point as I went on to explain to her the following. "This is like being a creative five-year old, cutting and pasting and doing 'show and tell.' In fact, I often feel like I'm back in kindergarten whenever I do this demonstration. You get to make it up using your own creative child inside you." She got the picture and had fun with the process.

Here are some examples where using this "billboard" for my subconscious worked beautifully!

In 1972, my first wife, Nancy, and I wanted to go on a vacation to Tahiti at Club Med. I walked through all the above steps, and the money I put on the poster was $2,400, the costs calculated for the trip. We then tacked the treasure map up on the living room wall where we could see it every day. At the time, $2,400 for a vacation was a great deal of money, and definitely not in the cards for our existing income.

Well, an amazing thing happened. In less than two weeks, there came in the mail a refund check from the IRS for overpayment of taxes. We had no idea this money was coming our way! My wife and I enjoyed a delightful vacation in Tahiti one month later.

Now, our son, David, thought this was a really cool idea because he had seen it work in action! So, he decided to make a treasure map with all the things he wanted at the time. For a twelve-year old with few opportunities for employment, this was definitely a stretch. To my amazement, within a few months, David had manifested everything on his treasure map that he had wanted. I had to admit that this seemed to work much faster for kids than adults. My guess was that he believed wholeheartedly this was going to work!

Some years later, I was doing some consulting work with a client. His office was near Seattle and he was in the business of potatoes, which took him over the mountains to the eastern part of the state a great deal of the time. His greatest challenge was flying over the mountains in a light plane unable to handle bad weather. I asked him how he thought he might solve this problem. He knew if he could purchase an airplane with greater power and better instruments, he would have no trouble. I asked him whether he had a clear picture of this plane. He told me he had a picture of one tucked away in his file cabinet.

Even though he was a skeptic, I suggested we try something I believed would work. I said, "Take that photo and place it right over your desk so that every day your subconscious mind will take a mental picture of you having this plane." Within one month, he called and said, "It's a miracle! I now own the airplane that was in the picture!"

In 1982, I met my present wife, Jane. On our first date, when I went to pick her up at her apartment, there on her walls were about 8–10 treasure maps of what she wanted to create in her life ranging from specifics in her spiritual life to all relationships, homes, business results, vacations, etc. I was greatly impressed at the adventurous dreamer she was, and excited to meet a fellow "treasure mapper."

After we had been dating a little over a year, one day she showed me a most unique treasure map. It included everything she had wanted in a committed relationship, in a marriage. It had adjectives like "spontaneous, adventurous, loving, fun, exciting, mutually fulfilling, respectful, great sex"…and others. Of course, I was into it, but what caught my eye right off the bat was at the very top, above a photo of me, were the words, in large print, **"Jack…or Better"**! Well, this treasure mapping was now working overtime because it was this simple phrase that actually pulled me up short and helped me get serious with my own process of determining what I really wanted. It didn't take long for me to realize that it was Jane all along!

The phrase "this…or better" is something that Jane has taught me a lot about over the past twenty-seven years. It is imperative not to set goals for other people when doing "treasure mapping." And the other fact is that when you focus on the vision (marriage), and not the process (a specific individual), you are automatically opening yourself up to the best possible choices that will fulfill the vision.

Every business I have started began with some form of creative visualization process. Can you imagine constructing a building without an architectural rendering? The problem I have with most architectural drawings is that they rarely include a large number of people in their sketches. Some intelligent architects have figured that one out.

Before I began any retail business, I always, and I mean always, pictured a waiting line to get in. It worked every single time. With The Blue Banjo, we had waiting lines wrapping around the block every single weekend. With Farrell's Ice Cream Parlours, we always had lines on the weekends, long lines of customers just waiting to get in. And with the Breadline Restaurant and Soup Kitchen, we sometimes had lines of customers winding around the corner down the block just waiting for our chicken and dumpling dinner on Sundays.

Remember this - Treasure mapping works, especially when you make it creative and fun.

Treasure mapping seems to be a more exciting way to play at business or anything in life. It is not the only way to advertise to your subconscious what you wish to create for there is no "right way" to do this. It is just one more very effective tool to use in practicing the creative process.

One psychological study found that only about 2% of adults in America use any creativity in their professional business, and daily life. This is compared to 10% of our seven-year olds. When five-year olds were tested regarding the usage of creativity, it was more than 90%! What happens during this period is that we become so imbalanced using the linear side of our brain that we allow the creative side of our brain to become atrophied. Like any muscular system, introducing new structures of repetitive use into our daily lives will restore healthy usage and great results!

Treasure mapping is a five-year old exercise. Use it often and it will enable you to become more creative in every area of your life.

At one time, I had 120 people in a treasure mapping workshop cutting and pasting, and then after one hour, we had everyone involved with show-and-tell. It was great fun watching this room of adults, some very "proper," transform into a room full of creative five-year olds!

Remember –

Creating and running your own business can be this much FUN!

CHAPTER 5

STORYBOARDING

In 1976, I attended a one-day seminar conducted by Michael Vance. This event was an affirmation to me that all the right-brain thinking and idea-generation that I had been engaging in over the years had been a most worthwhile endeavor.

Michael Vance had spent many years as head of Idea Development for Walt Disney Productions, Disneyland and Walt Disney World. The major idea I came away with at this FUN-filled lecture was the concept of storyboards.

Walt Disney, early on, had developed the "storyboard idea" as a way to see the whole picture while he was creating an idea. Michael Vance said the employees would tack/pin ideas on a wall as they would come up. He mentioned that Walt Disney's wife had been a little upset as the newly painted walls in his office were being destroyed with so many holes as the ideas were never-ending!

The animators loved the concept because it made easy the process of inserting ideas and sketches into the mix as stories were evolving. They had school children coming in on weekends to contribute as well, and this became such a success that some children were being rewarded large sums of money; they were very good at idea-generation. And why not? Disney was alert to the fact that these were his customers. These six, seven and eight-year olds were the ones talking their parents into buying!

The storyboard idea became so popular that one of the first things the movie industry does now when creating a movie is to sketch out each scene before shooting. These sketches, in most cases, are stick figures. No more than five or ten minutes are invested at this stage in any given scene, and this saves the production team tremendous sums of money.

So, why not use this technique in creating a business? That was my first thought after attending Michael Vance's seminar. Within months, I was attaching corkboards to my rented office space. I had been thinking of creating a fast-food, healthy restaurant and thought it would be fun to storyboard it. Since storyboarding can save time and money, I gave myself three months, ninety days, until I was open and running. Not having a location or the money, or even the menu, this was a daunting challenge indeed.

I started on December 1, 1976, and opened March 7, 1977, ninety-seven days total. I was seven days late, but that's not half bad when you're starting from zero. Here's how it happened, and at every step, I was giving thanks for the storyboard concept which made it happen.

First, I pinned up 3x5 index cards with all the tasks that had to be done: financing, menu, location, types of employees, promotions, advertising, store layout, unique factors, logo, colors, dishes, equipment, counters, tables and chairs, atmosphere, music, and decorations, just to name a few. These were put up randomly.

Then each of the idea cards in different colors started appearing on the board. I paid people $20/each to come to brainstorming sessions, with about thirteen sessions in all. I always made certain that a few potential customers were present, especially women because the women of the household were usually deciding whether and where the family was going to eat out. Within a few weeks, all the cards were in some sort of order as to when a task was to be completed, taking the project from start to finish. Now the story was beginning to take shape.

I was almost two months into this project and didn't really have a name yet. You know how things just don't come to you when you're trying too hard. I was driving to Portland to meet with my old partner, Joe, an investor in the project. When I was just passing through Centralia, the name came to me: **Yonny Yonson's Salad, Sandwich & Yogurt Shop.** It became so obvious as we had decided on the menu, and at that time not many people were eating frozen yogurt, let alone plain yogurt. Besides, the word "yogurt" didn't even sound appetizing. So I thought we would need a name to lighten things up.

Back in North Dakota where I grew up, in Boy Scout Camp, every summer we would sing *"My name is Yonny Yonson, I come from Wisconsin, I work in the lumber yard there ~ I walk down the street, all the people I meet ask me how did I come to be there ~ And I tell them ~ My name is Yonny Yonson ~ "* The song is sung in a round style, over and over again. That day, the song I sang when I was twelve popped right into my head, and our restaurant chain was born. Within a few years, there were six Yonny Yonson's.

The storyboard was a blessing and gave the project impetus. Every day I could just look on this board and see the whole picture taking shape in one glance. When a task was completed, I would move it over to the "finished" column. I didn't seem to be stressed as the business I was creating was in fact creating itself on the wall. And true to the creative process, every idea created energy for action steps, every action step completed generated energy for the next ones to follow, creating a momentum to our completion. This was a big wall 8x10 ft. and the storyboard took up the entire space. I find that the mind works like a computer sorting all the cards in the perfect order without confusion, organically.

When starting any new business idea, project or a new division within a company, use the storyboard idea and let go of the process. Let go of which step should go where and watch the organic magic of the creative mind at work. Trust me ~ there is a communication and a synergy that goes on between the right and left brains that when we allow it to work, will perform feats far greater than one could ever imagine using just one or the other alone.

This very book is being storyboarded as I write it. All the chapters and ideas are moving around weekly and structuring themselves in the best possible order. It's actually fun watching a storyboard change. It becomes alive, an organic project in action, and you really don't want it to end. The FUN after all is in the journey. My storyboard has become such a good friend that a part of me will miss it. The great news is that the completion of this storyboard will generate energy into the next project and storyboard.

When creating anything new with storyboarding, you no longer need to be concerned with the forgetting of a good idea, or leaving something out, and that alone will help you sleep better at night when you're working on those projects!

Incidentally, Yonny Yonson's made money the first month we were in business, and continued on for some seventeen years while we sold sandwiches, salads, soups and frozen yogurt to the greater Seattle area.

CHAPTER 6

TENSION-RESOLUTION SYSTEMS IN BUSINESS

In the last chapter, I discussed how to create storyboards, making it easy to see the whole project at one glance. What I did not mention is the unseen forces that help to bring about the end result.

In our every day life, we constantly create what we want in all kinds of small ways throughout the day. While I'm at work, I feel hunger pangs, and immediately two or three restaurants come to mind. My mind has automatically set up a tension-resolution system. No. 1: Know where I am at ~ sitting at my desk feeling hungry; No. 2: I picture the end result of the restaurant I am going to visit. I travel to the restaurant usually with very little conscious thought of how to get there. I have now resolved the tension, while minor, of ending my hunger.

Using this principle, found in Robert Fritz's book, *The Path of Least Resistance*, is of the utmost importance in creating a successful business. *"It is a principle found throughout nature that tension seeks resolution. From the spider web to the human body and from the formation of galaxies to the shifts of continents, we see tension-resolution systems."* Doing it consciously, on a regular basis, with large and small projects will enhance your creativity 100 times.

Here is how I used this principle to create our restaurant establishment called Yonny Yonson's where we sold soups, salads, sandwiches and frozen yogurt for seventeen years. When I go to the mall and I am headed to the electronics store, the first thing I do is go straight to the directory board and look for the red dot that tells me where I am. This saves me from wandering around for a half hour looking for my destination. If I don't know where I am, it becomes very difficult to get to the place where I wish to wind up.

Sounds quite simple, but always remember this: In most cases, you will not end up where you want to be if you have no idea of your accurate starting point. No doubt you have heard the story that illustrates this point. If you are actually standing in Chicago, and wish to fly to New York, but believe you are in Seattle, you will wind up somewhere in the Atlantic Ocean as your destination. Why did you not end up in New York? Because you thought your starting point was in Seattle, you traveled the distance that actually exists between Seattle and New York, and consequently, you overshot your mark by many miles.

I watch this phenomena occur every day with business owners where not having accurate information of where you are at and where you want to go can have disastrous effects.

Here's an example of how I began to set up structural tension without even being aware of what I was doing. I was sitting in my office one day, wanting to create a healthy fast-food restaurant knowing full well that I did not have the funds to do it myself. I also had no clue of the ideal location or final menu at the time. Just beginning to visualize the end product of the healthy fast-food restaurant in mind, I was already setting up "structural tension." I knew where I wanted to end up in three months and I knew factually where I was at the time. With these two pictures held simultaneously in my mind, I was holding the unseen force ~ structural tension ~ that is the necessary element for all creativity.

This was far more important than knowing exactly "how" I was going to reach my goal: the process. Holding this picture of these two things, where I was at the current moment, and what I wanted, simultaneously, is the dynamic creation of structural tension. And over time, with every action step, the continued clarification of current reality and your end vision, this structural tension will automatically resolve itself. It is in the very nature of the physics of "structural tension" to do so.

Think of a wind-up top. What happens when you wind it up as far as it can go? It gets to a point where it must release and spin. The tension is resolved. Think of a rubber band that is stretched to the limit. What occurs when you release it? The physical tension resolves itself and it returns to its normal state.

Let's look at another example. How many of you have been to a fire walk?

Around 1984, I went to see what all the excitement was about concerning "fire walking." I went there to observe. After a two-hour seminar led by Tolly Burkin, I made a decision that I would walk on hot coals. Now, as an engineer, I knew very well that 2000-degree hot coals would in fact burn my feet, so I knew I had to think differently to accomplish what I was about to do.

I got in touch with my fear, my nervous knees and my thoughts that this was indeed crazy. At the same time, I focused on the outcome. I pictured myself on the other side with perfect feet and not one single burn. Now all of a sudden, it didn't matter how I got there. The process was no longer important. I did in fact end up on the other side unscathed and learning a valuable lesson. Don't get so hung up in the "how to" of anything. Rather focus on the outcome with all unrelenting intention.

When setting up a business project, you as the creative genius can use this process that nature has been teaching us from the beginning of time in order to accomplish huge goals. Start with the smaller projects and practice until you begin to feel more confident. Use some of the tools in this book in order to get to this place, and always remember, set-up is 95% of anything.

It is important to set big goals so you can create greater structural tension. I like to use the term "well-defined, long-range, impossible goals" as my set-up. And what I have been learning through the years is that it is the goals, the visions that in fact stretch us so that we can achieve the end result.

To clarify, we're not talking here about "psychological tension," but rather "structural tension," which is simply created with two different points of focus without knowing how you are going to resolve the tension. Another way of saying it might be that "structural tension" is the activity of creating focus on different points simultaneously, and "psychological tension" would be the feelings that may rise and fall about and during that activity. There will always be the element of letting go in the space between the two points, knowing that the "how to" or the "process" will become clear as you continue to be in touch with where you are as well as the final destination.

Perhaps you've heard the term, "Let go and let God." This is about trusting in yourself and allowing that Higher Power along with the creative genius within you to lead the way. Everything in life is practice, so here is a method to try out consciously what you have been doing unconsciously all of your life. The only difference is now you can accomplish your business projects with greater ease knowing that nature has already shown us the way.

Tension-resolution systems always work.

Try them out and then practice - practice - practice!

CHAPTER 7

GETTING EXCITED ABOUT YOUR WORK!

It was the beginning of spring, 1972, and I had just received a phone call during the dinner hour. Our young daughter, Lorrie, informed me it was long distance, and that it was Charlie Jones. I picked up the phone, and inquired, "Who is this?" The voice on the other end responded, "This is Charlie Tremendous Jones." Well, I had heard of Charlie Jones for years. We had most of his inspirational tapes in our office, and I had just finished reading his book, *Life is Tremendous*. But there was absolutely no reason why he would be calling me, so I inquired again, "Okay, who is this… really?" convinced it was Bob Farrell in Portland pulling a trick on me…again! The caller responded, "No, this is really Charlie Tremendous, and I would like to have breakfast with you guys from Farrell's."

Well, Charlie had just given a talk in Minneapolis to the Farrell employees, was now on his way to Hawaii to give another speech, and was on a two-hour layover in Seattle, Washington. Well, we did arrange to meet and it was surely the most fun two hours I'd spent in a long time!

After meeting with Mr. Jones, I went home and re-read his book. This chapter is my recap of how Charlie and his writings have inspired me ever since that day. In his book, Charlie refers to the Seven Laws of Leadership. I believe if you even just learn the first one, your life will start becoming more powerful.

The first law of leadership is <u>Learning to Get Excited About Your Work</u>. Charlie Jones always says that he hears folks saying, "Show me a man who will work, and I'll show you a success." His response, "Show me a man that will say that and I'll show you an idiot!" His point is that work in and of itself will not give anyone great results, but learning to get <u>excited</u> about your work will.

Through the years, people have often said to me, "You know, it's easy for you to get excited about what you're doing. After all, you're in a FUN business!" My partner and I had many professionals want to quit what they were doing and go into our business. Typical comments were, "I've always wanted to be in the restaurant business…it looks so easy!" And my quick response was, "You wouldn't be saying that if you had this lousy job of mine…I hate work!"

"Work" wherever you find it, often carries implications of details, monotony, preparation, striving, harried days, and weariness. And no matter how romantic a business idea may seem to others, all these things I will need to overcome no matter what I am doing. Now, getting excited about my work is the same as acting enthusiastic about what I am doing. It is important to act the part you want to be. Think, envision, the person you would like to be, daily take action steps to embody that, and eventually one day, you will wake up and discover that you have become that individual.

In the words of Dale Carnegie, "Act enthusiastic and you will become enthusiastic." If I have any task to do, and I say to myself, "I will act enthusiastically about this task," and then actually enlist my feelings of excitement about it, I will, without fail, eventually become enthusiastic about that specific task, job, project.

But I have to tell you, when I first heard about this concept, my belief system was that this was a bunch of hooey. I also know you cannot motivate any other person, only yourself. The following is a true story.

When we first went into the restaurant business (this could be true for any business), we had many young people working on our staff who, quite frankly, moved around like snails. Their minds were always on something other than their jobs. You remember what it was like to be a teenager, or maybe you're raising one or more as we speak.

I recall vividly one certain busboy; let's call him "Wayne." Wayne wasn't able to spot a dirty table even if he was sitting on top of one. His head was up in the clouds, in the back room, in the freezer, outside…everywhere else but doing his job, which was bussing tables. One day, I mentioned to him, "Wayne, we are going to get excited about your work!" (Notice the "we") "When a party leaves their table, I'm going to holler out, 'DT34' for dirty table #34, third row over and fourth table in that row. When you hear that, you're going to get so excited about clearing that table that you won't be able to think of anything else."

Well, I don't consider myself a hypnotist, but a funny thing happened from that moment on: Wayne moved so fast, his mind had to move faster to catch up with his body. His adrenaline started pumping, and from then on we couldn't slow Wayne down! He became one of our fastest, most exceptional busboys of all time!

In fact, my partner, Joe, came on shift one night and was watching Wayne, his eyes darting here and there, on the prowl for the next DT. Joe inquired, "Wayne, what in the world are you doing?" Excitedly, Wayne informed him with all the gusto of a man on a mission, "I'm looking for DT's!" See what getting excited does ~ it gets the job done!

One day, I had a five-foot long fancy frame hung in our office, and the sign read, "Act enthusiastic and you'll be enthusiastic." A visual like this, when it starts to catch on, watch out! When all your key people get excited about what they are doing, it spreads like wildfire. It will keep all your employees coming back to work, enthusiastically, every single day.

A wonderful book on this subject, written by Norman Vincent Peale, is *Enthusiasm Makes the Difference.* I have purchased more than 100 copies of this book, giving them as gifts to many of my employees. I don't know how many actually read the book, but I do recall on one occasion, about ten years later, one of my former employees reported, "You know, I just finished reading that book you gave me, and it was great!" One never knows once a seed is planted, where or when it will take root and sprout.

An important lesson I've learned through the years is this. Regardless of one's good intentions to inspire and motivate, enthusiasm is something that has to originate from the inside of a person; it can only be encouraged from its source, inside oneself. Just as cynicism is habitual, so, too, is enthusiasm. The word "enthusiasm" has its origin in the Greek word "enthousiasmos" derived from "en" (in), and "theos" (God).

Charles Schwab once said, *"A man can succeed at almost anything for which he has unlimited enthusiasm."* Emerson concurred, *"Enthusiasm is the mother of effort, and without it, nothing great was ever accomplished."*

Here are four simple steps to support you in getting excited about your work:

1. Get excited about ideas.

Ideas originate from thoughts, feelings, imagination. They are the impulses inspiring us to create reality from <u>un</u>seen possibilities; what can be. They are the juice, the inspiration that causes us to make choices to do what we are most afraid to do, inspiring us to move outside our old comfort zones. Ideas are an act of will, regardless of the feelings surrounding them. The more choices we make, the less fear that occurs in trusting those ideas, which generates greater confidence in allowing unlimited creativity in our ideas, continuing through to completion.

2. Learn to get excited about obstacles.

Every single problem, challenge, obstacle to every single idea is only an opportunity for growth, and greater creativity...no matter what!

3. Learn to become/think like a child.

The adult in us continually worries about the outcome. But I guarantee you that there is a four-year old in you with the potential to be excited about each and every moment of every day. Nurture her/him; give her/him opportunities daily to "play" with creativity/ideas while the critic/judge is on vacation.

4. Learn to get excited about goal setting.

Practice dreaming about, writing down BHG's: Big, Hairy Goals! The most fun is in the actual journey on your way to living the dreams, walking the goals, and the bigger the goal/dream/vision, the more FUN you will have!

If you have any doubts about whether any of this makes sense, I would suggest you just try it for one week, and observe where it takes you. Pay attention to the energy you have in your mind, body and spirit. Notice any differences in how you feel, your responses to everyone in your life, and their responses toward you. Observe the energy you have at the end of the day. Keep a journal for that one week. I guarantee you it will be one of the most fun weeks you've had in a long time!

Samuel Goldwyn once said, "*No person who is enthusiastic about his work has anything to fear from life.*"

I remember the day I was asked to give a talk to the Winner's Circle breakfast. This was back in the early 1980's. There was a group of some 200 business professionals who met every Tuesday morning at 7:00 a.m. At first, I thought how scary this would be. In fact, I thought of ten reasons right off the bat for why I really had no business giving this speech.

When I got home, I decided to do something different. I took out a piece of paper and wrote down spontaneously, in no particular order, all the things I could share with this audience. Within thirty minutes, I was beginning to feel excited about how much fun it would be to give this presentation. My enthusiasm took over, and I gave a tremendous talk that morning entitled, "Do What You're Afraid to Do!" That morning, I remembered speaking about my feelings of fear and what I went through in trying to talk myself out of this experience. I had thirty-six people (yup, I counted them!) telling me afterwards what a great speech it was, and it took at least that many before I began to accept that I had done a professional job.

Nowadays, when fear rears its ugly head, I just remember to get excited about what I have been asked to do. The enthusiasm begins to overcome any fear that might exist, and then I just move into the energy, one action step at a time.

I remember when my good friend, Dan Riley, received a promotion at his job. He was an engineer and we had discussed this subject in length. First off, Dan went out and bought himself two brand new suits. He wanted to dress the part he was about to play. Every day he went to work deciding he would play the part he would become.

After one week, something unusual started happening which convinced Dan that he really was on the right track. Several employees in the company started coming up to him to ask him questions just as if he were the manager of the department. It wasn't long before Dan moved to the next level and became manager. The dream he had held in his imagination had now become a reality!

This scenario is no different than getting a character role in a play. You act the part, practice it over and over again, until you become the character, and it becomes an integral part of who you are.

Becoming excited about your work is really not that difficult. Remember to start playing the part before you get on stage. In other words, start going over your part at least one hour before you show up at work. You have absolutely nothing to lose!

CHAPTER 8

BRAINSTORMING ~
THE IDEA-GENERATION GAME

Why make brainstorming a game? Because you have strict guidelines to ensure its success, you get to use imaginary money and most of all, it's FUN! Creative juices always flow easier with the element of FUN mixed in.

In the early 1980's, I was hired to conduct a brainstorming session to come up with the name for a new restaurant establishment being built in the Madison Park area of Seattle. It was to be an upscale, healthy establishment with lots of salads and fresh garden vegetables. When I arrived, there were some twenty-six people in attendance. I wondered how on earth I was going to manage this large of a group for brainstorming knowing that this kind of thing generally works best with five to eight individuals. Thank goodness, they had access to a copy machine to run off the rules I had brought with me, and we began with our goal to come up with a minimum of 100 ideas in one hour for the new restaurant name.

Surprisingly, it all worked to perfection, and we came up with 146 ideas for the restaurant's name in the allotted time. By the time we had narrowed it down to ten, the winner was obvious, and the new restaurant was christened, ***Madison Square Garden.***

Before the 1980's, I didn't really have a set of rules or guidelines for brainstorming. We would just sit around with usually three or four friends, and think up new and different businesses to start. It was really around 1973 that I began learning how powerful regular brainstorm sessions could be.

I observed some interesting phenomena surrounding this activity. Two people could come up with perhaps twenty ideas in an hour, but when we added a third, that amount jumped to 100 or more. I've never figured out why, but I do know it works, and it works every single time! Every Friday, for four months, I would gather three or four individuals, including myself to brainstorm on the following idea***: How do I create a million-dollar restaurant with $100,000 startup capital that will appeal to the masses?*** The million dollars was what we would gross in one year. The $100,000 startup was the amount I would receive from selling my share in another operation.

One of the people in this group was to create the recipes and manage the kitchen. For this, he received 10% of the equity in the business. Another person was a banker and the third, who attended intermittently, was an advertising executive.

I can recall the day we came up with the name, ***The Breadline Restaurant.*** It was perfect because we had figured out we would be selling soup and bread in a 1930's atmosphere and wanted the vision to be people lined up a block long excitedly waiting to be seated. All this brainstorming paid off when ***The Breadline & Soup Kitchen*** opened its doors in 1974 in a basement in the old section of Seattle; we had enormous lines just waiting to get in to our 300-seat, Depression-era bread and soup kitchen. Here's the story of what happened.

Since we would be serving soup and bread at lunch (only six choices), we decided that all our servers could be senior citizens—one of the first things that made us truly unique. The choice for dinner was beef or chicken stew; $1.25 for lunch and $3.25 for dinner. Other items that truly set us apart, making us a destination place as a restaurant were the following:

- A Model-A-Ford truck set in the center of the restaurant piled high with homemade bread.

- Ten "Kitchen Queens" from the 1920's were displayed throughout the restaurant.

- The bar was known with signage, as ***The Filling Station*** complete with old gas pumps, headlamps and fenders from 1930's automobiles, with tractor seats at the bar.

- Beer was served in old Kerr jars and wine was served in old milk bottles; water was served in old Mason canning jars.

- All workers' uniforms were bright-colored 1930's attire.

- Lots of old tin advertising signs, some purposely distressed, were hanging throughout the bar and restaurant.

- Old ads were painted on the brick walls.

- The menu was written with chalk on blackboards around the restaurant.

- The servers were allowed to offer seconds, spontaneously, without it being advertised to enhance the experience of being at Grandma's house for dinner.

- Fresh homemade pies were made in an open kitchen along with the bread and soup, and their aroma filled up the restaurant and poured out onto the sidewalk.

- All the light fixtures were wash buckets turned upside down, hung from the ceiling.

- Two percent of our budget went into fresh cut flowers twice a week, and for plants and vines hanging from the ceiling using grow lights at night.

- None of the chairs and tables matched; they were all rustic. We built a forty-foot long wooden table anchored into the floor that people loved to sit at, especially during lunch. Definitely a "community connection" item.

- While customers were waiting to be seated at their tables, they were reading 1930's magazines and listening to the finest music from that era.

- The daytime bartender was my dad. He had just turned ninety-one when he started, and worked every day until retiring at ninety-five years old!

The most creative brainstorming idea we had was to print up certificates for four dinners good for a period of one year. My goal was to raise $100,000 before we even opened the doors. My friend, Gertrude Popp, now a most successful restaurant owner and caterer on her own in Seattle, contacted all the charities in town to see whether they wanted to raise money for their organizations selling our dinner certificates. In fact, we raised $72,000 and split with the charities that took it on. The promotion benefit outweighed the money we took in! As a result, we now had 24,000 people who knew about our restaurant and were coming to dinner, and all this before we had ever opened the doors for one meal! This was at a discount price of $3.00 instead of $3.25.

The second most creative promotion we did was to open with 1929 prices with all the products paid for by our suppliers. Then we could have a pre-opening practice session. We did this for three nights and created such long lines that the *Seattle Times*, having got wind of this, came down just to take pictures and ended up giving us an eight-page feature spread in its Sunday magazine pictorial section. Within a few weeks, most everyone in the city knew we had arrived, and serving 1,000 or more meals daily became the norm.

By the end of 1974, we had been open for ten months and were approaching our million dollar goal when we sold the concept to a group that was planning to take the concept nationwide. My plan was to retire with royalties coming in for at least the next ten years.

The buyers built a store in Vancouver B.C., and proceeded to lose $400,000 over a three-year period. I was asked, after one year, to go up to their establishment and see what went wrong. Within minutes of entering the restaurant, it was apparent that they had decided to save money, excluding implementing many of the fourteen unique items mentioned above that had made the original concept so successful. To cut costs, they used maybe only half of the items, and therefore, had limited themselves to only half of the strengths that had made the concept fly upon opening in Seattle.

Our food costs were hovering around 28%, and they thought they could lower it even further. They cut out fresh flowers, bright-colored uniforms, and a number of other significant items. We had some fifty senior citizens working for us; they employed fifteen. They also made the error of advertising seconds on their menu instead of offering them spontaneously as we had. There were several other changes they made, all of which contributed to stripping the original concept of what made it work in the first place. A great example of the law: if it's not broken, why fix it?

I have no regrets in that the fun was in the journey, and it was a great and wonderful creative journey. And I learned how the exercise of brainstorming can work wonders.

In fact, given the current economy and what we have gone through as a country, I am convinced that this concept would be extremely valuable today. So, if you're reading this book, and it strikes you as something you would like to do, give me a call (info in back of the book). I'm always looking for talented and experienced individual(s) who can run the show (aren't afraid of work), and I will provide the consulting/mentoring to make sure it stays on track as a profitable venture. A destination eatery of this kind would accomplish several needs in the marketplace (a benchmark for any new establishment).

✓ **One** ~ It would provide simple, nutritious foods at lower prices due to the simplicity of the menu.

✓ **Two** ~ It would employ and nurture great numbers of senior citizens, many of whom have lost their retirement and need to work both for financial reasons and to continue to be viable, contributing individuals of value in the marketplace.

✓ **Three** ~ It would provide an energy of hope providing a powerful reminder with all the Depression era paraphernalia, menus, environment, etc., that we came through those tough times of the Depression, and created something stronger as a nation…and we can do it again.

I would welcome speaking with any interested parties. Who knows what might be around the bend?!

Moving on ~

I mentioned earlier "imaginary" money. In the setup of brainstorming sessions, I always like to add an amount of money to the question we are addressing, even though the money doesn't yet exist in reality. *For example: For a $10,000 investment, how do I sell 100,000 copies of this book in the FWP?*

(FWP...Fastest Way Possible)

Here's another ~ ***For $5,000, how do I create a business that I would love, is an expression of who I am, and engages all my strengths and talents in the FWP?*** Now, you don't need to possess the $5,000 when you start this session; just putting in the specific amount will help stimulate the ideas you will need to convince a friend or lender that this is really a great business. I mentioned earlier how I spent $500 to have a set designer create artistic drawings of the breadline, and how beneficial this was as I was marketing this idea to bankers and others. These drawings contained the bulk of the ideas we had brainstormed on earlier, and were now in living color.

Over the years, I have been exploring and learning what elements assist in creating a most powerful brainstorming session. The following is the result of that evolution:

Brainstorming Rules:

1. Write the problem in the form of a question in one sentence, and add "FWP" (Fastest Way Possible).

2. Put value (risk) to the problem. What are you willing to invest, give, in order to create the solution? Here you can use imaginary money.

3. Allow a maximum of ninety minutes ~ RELAX AND HAVE FUN!

4. Go for 100 ideas in one hour.

5. Make no judgments as ideas are contributed, good or bad (total acceptance).

6. Any idea is acceptable ~ make thinking outside the box the norm.

7. Write all ideas down.

8. Hitchhike on ideas.

9. Once the 100 ideas are down, select ten ideas from the list by having each individual select his or her five favorites.

10. Choose one idea from the ten meeting this criteria:

- Easy to follow through
- Most effective
- Requires least amount of resources; time/ energy/monies

Suggestions for Facilitator

A. To speed up the process, when someone is elaborating on a complex idea, write it down and suggest returning to it later.

B. When stuck, expand (worldwide) or contract (think smaller unit…family, local community).

C. Halfway through the session, add a sense of urgency: ***"If we only had one day, what would we do?"***

Give this a try and add to or use parts of it as you see fit. After all, it is a practice that is still evolving. Remember, strict guidelines with the addition of imaginary money always amps up the energy and FUN to any game!

I still own the Breadline Concept after going through a litigation that was settled out of court. In fact, the last statement of the arbitrator to the purchasers was something to the effect, "If you entered into an agreement to invest all these monies for something this unique, why would you then set about to change the very elements that were ensuring the success of this establishment in the first place?" My thoughts exactly!

I don't carry any regrets regarding that time. And, I do have the knowledge of using my creative abilities to the max during that period, and am most grateful for the whole experience.

CHAPTER 9

PARTNERS: DO I REALLY NEED A BUSINESS PARTNER?

Let's explore the importance of having a partner in business. From the years 1938 to 1940, I was six to eight years of age. Even at those tender years, I somehow knew that it was going to be much easier to sell corn and eggs door-to-door with a partner than without one.

Just two blocks away from our home, in Minot, North Dakota, lived one of my friends, Joey Rutten, a few years younger than me. Right off the bat, I enlisted Joey to be a partner with me selling the produce my dad grew on a small farm on the outskirts of town. We sold eggs and corn for ten cents/dozen, and we got to keep all the money! Little did I know that some twenty-five years later, Joe and I would hook up again in Seattle, Washington and venture out as business partners in our Farrell's franchise adventure.

I had attended Seattle University and had received a degree in civil engineering. Joe went to Gonzaga and obtained his college degree in accounting. After college, we both ended up working at The Boeing Company. After I had opened The Blue Banjo Night Club, Joe saw that I was having a lot more fun than he ever had working at Boeing, so he asked whether he could join me in a business partnership at The Blue Banjo. We eventually opened two more businesses in the same area, but neither was as successful as The Blue Banjo. We even called one of them our "$10,000 wind tunnel" as it was a great learning experience for both of us.

When we opened our first Farrell's Ice Cream Parlour Restaurant, we did a very wise thing. We took a sheet of paper, drew a line down the middle, and divided up the responsibilities we would be sharing in running our establishment. Joe's side included anything relating to the handling of money, lease negotiations, insurance, purchasing, hiring cashiers, fountain and kitchen staff. My side included anything relating to promotion, marketing/advertising, construction, maintenance, signage, interior design/décor and the hiring of waiters and busboys.

Each of these tasks involved a certain level of skill and we both were on a very steep learning curve without which we knew we would probably be out of business in less than a year. The first six months we were each working and learning at a rate of about 80–100 hours/week. Most people don't realize that in order to be successful in any business, it will often require as much study and training as it would in order to be a surgeon or a lawyer. Of course, one is studying a different area of expertise; nevertheless, it can be just as grueling and demanding as the other. There are no shortcuts in being a seasoned successful entrepreneur.

There is another element that is of the utmost importance. It would be what Michael Phillips refers to as "tradeskill" in his book *Honest Business*. He refers to tradeskill as the most important attribute anyone can have in business. It is not the same as "business ability." "Tradeskill" would be a word to describe the innate qualities that make one individual more effective than another in starting and operating successfully a small business.

I didn't realize it when I quit my career as a Boeing engineer and opened my business that since both my parents had been entrepreneurs in their own ventures, I already had a significant advantage in creating a successful business. My father had created and operated a successful meat market in Minot, ND. My mother was always creating different kinds of crafts and always sold them for significant profits. Even when I was very small, my mother would run a food stand at the State Fair every summer, and I was right there as her number one assistant. Even back in those early days,

I was absorbing the ways of becoming a successful creative entrepreneur.

On a scale of 1–10, Michael Phillips would give me a 10 simply because running a business was a natural element of my everyday life due to the entrepreneurial ways of both my parents. If only one parent has been an entrepreneur, you would receive a "6." So what if neither parent, nor any other family member has ever operated his or her own business… are you doomed for failure? Absolutely not! Take heart. There are some simple choices you can make to compensate.

Some fifteen years ago, I met John Avinger, whose parents were both schoolteachers. He is the owner and operator of John's Music Store in the Wallingford District in Seattle. He was really struggling to stay afloat. Since John sold drums made in countries all around the world, and I also loved drumming, it made sense to both of us that I become John's business mentor. We met on a regular basis for a couple of years until he had developed the tradeskills to carry on alone.

As of this writing, John's Music Store has been going now for some twenty-six years with no end in sight! When we met, every month looked like his last. I can honestly say that John has taught me through the years as much as I have been able to teach him.

Having someone who can lead you and mentor you through all the ups and downs of running a business is of utmost importance. In the book, *Honest Business*, it states:

"There are several alternatives to consider if you don't have tradeskills: You can go ahead (and probably fail), you can find a partner, get special training or find a boss."

I would add one other thing and that is to hire a mentor or coach who is business savvy. It is far too difficult to go it alone unless you have no employees and you are working independently…and even then, it can be most challenging.

Your partner could be what we call a "silent partner," usually one who puts up the money, and with whom you can meet on a regular basis. The most important thing would be making sure your partner knows more about creating a successful business than you do, or the person won't be much benefit to you in the long run.

What is wrong with not having a partner? Well, it could mean that your idea was not good enough to attract even your own friends who know you best.

Let me say it again ~ Starting a business and causing it to thrive is difficult for one person to go it alone. In my own case, I needed someone who was present and available to talk me out of some dumb decision I was on the verge of making. I needed someone to bounce ideas around with and mostly, I needed someone to cheer me on when things got tough and were going south.

It is not much different than being in a marriage. Select your business partner wisely, with the same care and consciousness as you would your spouse. Joe and I stayed partners for seventeen years. Oh, sure, we had many arguments and differences along the way, but being in alignment with a common vision and goal with separate responsibilities being clearly designated helped us to stay the course. I have had other more powerful and less powerful partners through the years, but when all is said and done, the partnership with my boyhood friend was probably the one where I learned the most and was by far the most fulfilling for me. Thanks, Joe!

Look at all the great businesses listed in Jim Collins' book, *Built to Last*, that were founded with complementary partners: Walt Disney, HP, Procter & Gamble, Marriott, Nordstrom, and now Microsoft.

If you don't have a partner in your business at this time, write down the characteristics and the skills needed to be your partner. It is sort of like marriage…opposites do attract. The things that are not easy for you, or that you don't enjoy doing are exactly the skills and attributes that your business partner needs to possess.

Go hunting and be open to finding that great and long-lasting business partnership.

SECTION TWO

OPEN FOR BUSINESS

Now What do I do?

CHAPTER 10

MONEY...MONEY...MONEY

...the three most important things when starting a business! And here you thought it was location...location... location! It's true, money is important, but not nearly as important as what we have talked about in the previous chapters. You have probably guessed by now that there is a progression to the startup and opening of a business. It is my opinion that the order of chapters in this book is the order in which you progress to the next stage in your business development.

I have discovered there are thousands of ways to create the capital for your business. Have you thought of them all? Fifty years ago I was convinced I knew all of them. During the past five decades, I've had to come up with many creative ideas to fund a business, and each time it has been a different solution.

We covered brainstorming in a previous chapter which illustrated how we can create money when there isn't any. The obvious sources are friends, venture capital, lenders, future suppliers and family.

In 1974, before I even opened The Breadline Restaurant, I wondered how on earth I could ever begin to raise $100,000 never having done anything like this. We did end up raising over $72,000 with pre-selling dinners. We covered the "how to" in an earlier chapter. For now, I want to illustrate that if you can think outside of the box, creating the money you need and want is not going to be as difficult as you might think.

At one time in our early career, Joe and I hired an astute businessman named August Pantages. The plan was to meet up with him on a weekly basis. We were struggling, and not seasoned enough at this time in order to secure a bank loan. We offered him $15/week, which was a stretch for us at the time. We met with our new mentor weekly, and during this time, he would coach us on the action steps to acquiring a $2,000 loan, including introducing us to a loan officer at The Bank of California.

Of course, he wanted us to succeed as he was also one of our suppliers. I had just turned thirty the day before we got the loan, and it was one of the happiest business days of my life. I don't think he ever cashed those $15 checks.

I remember reading a book, also by Michael Phillips, entitled *The Seven Laws of Money*. I have never forgotten the first law: "If you are doing the right thing, the money will come." This statement has proven itself to me many times over. When asking for the money, there is definitely a less and a more powerful way to go about it.

In 1982, I was teaching a series of classes I created called "Money Unlimited." Each course lasted for eight weeks, and my friend, Sheila Connor, became a partner with me in the marketing and co-teaching of these classes. We eventually completed seventy eight-week workshops with ten to twelve participants in each class.

Part of the teaching was to role-play the activity of asking for money, a job, a bank loan, or whatever else each wanted to create the coming week. Rather than saying, "I would like," "I need," "Would it be too much trouble," "Is it okay...," each participant would practice saying, "I want..." with conviction, without smiling, and in a powerful, direct manner. You couldn't fake it as the whole class could tell immediately whether you spoke with conviction. It was no different than an acting class where you have to practice owning the character you are portraying.

One of the ideas I had was to have each person carry a $100 bill on his person during the week so that when he went into a store, he would not be able to resort to, "I don't have any money," or "I can't afford that."

One day, I decided to test myself and went into a bank to purchase a $1,000 bill. I went into the first bank and said to the person at the counter, "Do you have a $1,000 bill I could purchase?" The quick response was "No, they don't make them any longer." When I went into the second bank, I remembered what I had been teaching in our workshops, and said to the teller, "<u>I want a $1,000 bill...I want it in a week...call me when you have it</u>." That is all I said, and then I walked out. In less than one week, I had my $1,000 bill.

The point here is why do we act sheepish or helpless when asking for money? I believe this behavior is the number one reason why individuals are unable to receive financing of any kind.

In 1985, I was invited to be a citizen diplomat on a trip to the Soviet Union. At the time, I didn't have the extra $2,500 required for the trip, so I decided once again to put this more powerful way of asking to the test. I asked some thirteen individuals, including some strangers, for $100/each. This was not a loan. However, I did not ask for the money in a traditional way. Instead, I said clearly to each one, "I want $100. I am going on a trip to Russia and when I return, I will invite you to a party at my home where I will do a presentation with a slide show about the adventure."

I raised $1,100 in one week from twelve people, with my personal funds making up the difference. And upon my return, I kept my promise with a great party, slide show and presentation just for all my angel investors.

When I think back on all the bank loans we received, we could have saved a great deal of time going to multiple banks if I had only mastered this technique sooner. It seems simple enough now, but it definitely has been a learned practice. And as you practice it yourself, it will serve you greatly in whatever endeavor you choose to undertake.

Let's review how you will enlist others to give the money for your venture.

- Have a tremendous idea.

- Build a specific vision.

- Identify your core values ~ your business will be a reflection of both you and your values.

- Create a picture, a layout, a treasure map, so that you, and others, can get a clearer picture of the end result that is desired.

- Storyboard your vision so you can see all the steps in one glance.

- Clarify your big goal and where you are at any time – this creates a structural tension, the nature of which is to resolve the vision into reality.

- Find a partner who also shares your vision, and whose strengths complement your own strengths/weaknesses in business.

- Ready, set...go for the money! Ask friends and others whether you can practice with them; role-play before going to banks or angel investors. Some might say, "I want to see your business plan," and for this, I would refer you to the range of excellent books and courses on this specific subject.

When you say, "I want" with power and conviction, the person being asked will go all out to fulfill your request or to find someone who will. There were only three $1,000 bills in the largest bank in Seattle with over 100 branches, and at least three individuals went to work finding one of them. They were so proud of what they accomplished!

Begin practicing asking for the money on smaller projects. The next time you go into a store, remember to ask clearly for what you want...the size, color, price, and just observe what happens. Of course, you are asking courteously vs. a rude demand, but you are clearly letting the individual know exactly what you want and what you will be checking out in other stores. Then progress from there, working your way up to that million-dollar loan.

Money is simply "energy" sitting just waiting to be put to good use. On any given day, at least ten individuals will be asking to use that money. The person who ends up receiving the money that day will be the one who has been practicing and using the tools in being open to, and asking for that "green energy."

That person could very well be you!

CHAPTER 11

TEN UNIQUE FACTORS THEORY

It is my belief that if I have ten unique ideas built into my business, I will create an above-average success rate in my profitability. I call this my insurance policy for success. If I do this before I even start or open my business, it will give me a significant advantage over every other individual in my target market.

As similar-concept businesses in my immediate geographical neighborhood add some of the ideas I've incorporated, it becomes important to brainstorm, as in Chapter 8, to come up with even more unique factors giving your business a continual edge.

In the early 1970's, I made it a habit to ask business owners and especially restaurant creators what made them unique and special. I was always taken off guard by their answers. "Our service and our atmosphere..." and sometimes, "Our prices and our unique menu items…" were the answers often given. These answers are almost always common statements shared by all restaurant owners. In many cases, they just had not taken the time and energy to identify those variables that set them apart in their market, and sometimes they had just a few unique factors built in from the outset.

In Chapter 5 on "Storyboards," I told you how we developed the Yonny Yonson's concept. Here are the ten unique factors we built into the concept from the outset.

We started with this question: What are the ten most unique things about Yonny Yonson's that makes it different from any other restaurant in its market area?

1. Natural Foods ~ no soft drinks, no white bread. Almost all our products had no preservatives. We used fruits with no sugar added, unsalted nuts, carob in place of chocolate and featured healthful herbal teas.

2. Innovative frozen yogurt desserts.

3. Medium-size healthy sandwiches and salads.

4. Easy take-out. We made it simple to take out any order in bags or boxes. Example: Our box lunch specials.

5. No smoking ~ all stores were smoke-free zones; healthy foods deserved a healthy environment. NOTE> At the time, smoking was still allowed in most eateries.

6. Fast turnover ~ because of the limited number of items (six sandwiches and three salads), we ran a very fast, high turnover restaurant; no substitutions.

7. Fun place ~ bright colors, fresh flowers and plants, positive employees and healthy foods; this was designed to be a FUN place to eat and work.

8. Healthy feeling ~ We engineered a "healthy feeling" design into the very store atmosphere by stressing natural products and showing them up front where the customer could see them. Our employees all had the appearance of health and vitality.

9. Live flowers and potted plants throughout ~ a very unique item.

10. Hot natural toppings ~ Our most popular sundae, "Hot Yonson" supported the notion that people enjoy a hot and cold simultaneous taste experience in sundaes. And ours were made with no sugar.

At the time, we were so unique that many people drove ten to fifteen miles just to have lunch, making our new establishment a true destination place. Our investment was $50,000, and the first year, we made $50,000. How about that for a return on investment! A friend put in $10,000 for 20% ownership in the concept and received close to that amount each year for the first ten years.

I can't emphasize enough how important it is to take the time to come up with the unique ideas that bring success to your creation. This is a recipe for success in any business, large or small.

Within five years, other establishments were following suit with what was at that time a unique trademark of our business. It followed suit that we needed to bring in additional ideas for our continued success.

In business, it is of the utmost importance to be re-inventing yourself. I believe innovation should be allowed to flourish at all times. That is why the entrepreneurial spirit is essential to every business. Some large corporations have difficulty evolving unless they are allowing for the right-brain creative thinkers to integrate with the linear minds working at all levels of strategic development. This combination will be facilitating out-of-the-box ingenuity allowing all the "think energy" to flow throughout the organization.

Each month in our organizations, we had it set up so that whatever employee came up with the most unique idea for saving money, promoting our business or adding a new service was rewarded financially.

We also instituted a positive idea called "well days," which affirmed employees for staying healthy and showing up for work. If you showed up everyday for three months, you received a one-day paid vacation in the following quarter. There was no pay for sick days. The focus was on being well rather than being sick, and it worked. The majority of employees were consistently healthy and always on the job.

So, how do you become unique in ten areas? Use the brainstorm technique set forth in Chapter 8.

For $2,000

What ten things make my business unique? OR
What are ten ideas that will make my business unique!

For a large business, that amount could easily be $100,000...and well worth it!

Almost all businesses when starting out are doing something that is different and an improvement over previous similar enterprises. That is why they feel they can make a difference in the marketplace. This chapter is about making a conscious effort to set a goal of integrating no less than ten unique factors or more into your particular business. If you do this, you will be rewarded ten-fold. These edges, these unique factors come from the choices you make from your list of ideas.

I have used the following quote many times in my speeches:

"Capital isn't so important in business. Experience isn't so important in business. You can always get both of those things. What is important are ideas. If you have ideas, you have the main asset you need, and there isn't any limit to what you can do with your business and your life. They are any person's greatest asset ~ Ideas!" — **Harvey Firestone**

CHAPTER 12

BRINGING THE FUN INTO GROWING YOUR BUSINESS

In 1959, when I was twenty-seven years old, I created my first FUN business. It was called The Blue Banjo located in "The Skid Road" section of Seattle, Washington. This establishment had at its very core the element of FUN; FUN for me as creator, FUN for employees, and definitely FUN for our customers.

We played music so people could sing along with the band or at least, stomp their feet to the rhythm. We would play, "I've Been Working On The Railroad," at least three times every evening. We also made an effort in our seating to connect customers with other customers they did not know. This created a great synergy for additional FUN as the evening progressed.

By 1961, The Blue Banjo had the reputation of being the most FUN place to visit in all of Seattle. I discovered at the time that the more fun the customers were having, the less they were concerned about how much they were paying for the tab. In fact, our customers were having so much fun that they didn't even notice when we raised prices!

My focus was always on how we could make this even more fun. So we began brainstorming ideas. Some of the following ideas were those implemented making The Blue Banjo one of the most fun night establishments around.

Fred, our "Greeter and Seater" fellow, was selling garters along with our .25 cent popcorn basket. These originals were made by my mother and sold for $1.25, a high price for garters in 1961. Fred would stick a piece of white cardboard in the band of his straw hat (we all wore straw hats) with ten garters on it and a sign at the top with the price. To make it even more fun, whenever a guy purchased a garter for his lady, Fred would blow a whistle and holler, "Garter Sale!"

In most cases, the band was between numbers, so he would have the lady stand up on her chair, or on the top of the bar, and then Fred would install the garter complete with drum roll and slide whistle from the band. Eventually, we were selling seventy-five garters every night!

Our tuba player, Elroy, taped bright-colored silk tulips all around the opening of his upright tuba, and once or twice each evening, I would make a ritual of going over and pouring beer from a pitcher all over the tulips and into his instrument. Another fun thing was that we installed an "auga" horn used on submarines so that every time we played "Anchors Away," we would set the horn off and yell, "Dive! Dive!"

Whenever the band, made up of three banjos, tuba, piano and myself on drums, took a break every forty-five minutes, I would pull down this old window shade where I had printed the words "Kidney Break" with a picture of a huge red kidney bean.

Hopefully, you're beginning to get the idea. With every FUN idea integrated into the fabric of our business, we could charge more with no worry of losing customers. And at our one-year anniversary mark, we were the only tavern in town with a cover charge to get in while still drawing long lines of customers.

In 1965, we opened our first Farrell's Ice Cream Parlour Restaurant in Bellevue, Washington, the second of 145 stores nationwide. This was the start of a territorial franchise for my partner, Joe, and me, and a natural fit for us. The element of creating FUN in business had, by this time, become second nature to us, and was the foundation of the Farrell's concept. In fact, FUN became such a trademark of this business that the employees, on their own initiative, had buttons printed up with the words, ***"It's FUN to work at Farrell's."*** Now when was the last time you heard of any business having its employees do such a thing! We had thirty-six employees at the time, and our costs for hiring a new employee were automatically reduced by this simple button because most of the young people around wanted to work in a FUN place.

I remember the day I suggested that we charge $1.00 for a banana split. At the time, we were selling the item for .75 cents, already the highest price for a banana split in our geographical area. We ended up selling more at $1.00 than we ever did at .75 cents! Again, no one seemed to notice because the customers were having as much FUN as our employees. On your birthday, all the employees would gather around, sing "Happy Birthday," and bring a FREE sundae with a candle in it. Within a few years, we and the customers were celebrating, in four different locations, some 60,000 birthdays every year with a sizeable portion of FUN. With an average of six customers per birthday party, that is over 360,000 people, and a lot of ice cream customers!

Another "event" was when someone would order the "ZOO." One of the employees would come out playing a bass drum, and others would be carrying the "ZOO" on a stretcher. Now the "ZOO" had enough ice cream, toppings and whipping cream to feed at least ten people. Many customers were drawn in just to see the show! The "PIG TROUGH" was another humongous item serving several customers where all the staff would oink in unison while it was being delivered.

After four years in this business, we decided it was time to give out a questionnaire and take written tally on just what our customers thought of us. At the time, during the months of August, November, and December, at the largest regional shopping center near Seattle, we were serving over 3,000 people our hamburgers and ice cream every day. After only one week, we ended the survey with more than 5,000 responses. On almost every single page, there was the word **"FUN."** It was a huge confirmation of our hunch that we were not selling food or ice cream; we were selling **FUN!** That's when I had a gigantic banner installed on our office wall to remind us every day what this business was really all about. It read, *"This company sells FUN!"*

The question most frequently asked of me by entrepreneurs is: "Can you integrate…really…the element of FUN into <u>any</u> business?" I mean, there are financial planners, garbage collectors, accountants, any number of jobs that we normally do not think of as FUN. Nevertheless, my answer is a resounding "YES!" If your employees, and you, are having FUN, the stage is set for your customers automatically to have FUN. This starts with the giving of recognition to each of your workers, acknowledging them for their individual energies, ideas, skills and abilities. This has nothing to do with more salary or raises.

In fact, in all the major employee surveys done in the marketplace, an increase in salary or a raise is usually around #10 on the list of what keeps people showing up for work every day. One of the items at the top of the list is allowing employees to come up with more FUN ways to accomplish their work in an atmosphere of creativity and collaboration vs. competition.

As a business owner, the responsibility for creating this atmosphere and getting the ball rolling lies with you. Once you take the initiative, your employees will follow suit. Allowing them to make decisions on the lowest possible level will also contribute to their experience of being valued and important, and it is always more FUN to come to work for any employee when you feel valued and important.

Encouraging and allowing employees to set their own sales and work goals is probably the most important element you can build into the foundation of your business. It has worked every time I have used it and without exception, the employees' expectations and goals for themselves far exceeded what I would have selected for them. In addition, the end results set by them as a team were far greater than what I would have imagined individually.

There are 1000's of ideas that can be implemented to transform any business into a FUN business. Ideas no one has even thought of yet. Back in 1991, I began a painting contracting business with the logo, ***"We Love to Paint!"*** To this day, some seventeen years later, if any employee doesn't have FUN painting, they don't work as an employee with our company.

In summary, here is a list of my personal criteria for a **FUN** place to work:

- Lots of praise and acknowledgement

- Know what is expected…goals of the business are clear

- Teachable atmosphere…a "Learning" organization encourages questions

- Employees are respected in word and deed

- Personal values are in alignment with business values

- Rewards given for exceptional work

- Opportunities to be creative and to grow in and with the company

- All individuals are included in the decisions affecting them

- Employees feel they are part of the company's overall decision-making process

- Opportunities to disagree

- Responsibilities are commensurate with skills/abilities

- Engaged in satisfying work

- Work culture/environment is an optimistic/positive one

- Sense of humor is encouraged

- There is an experience of integrity, opportunities for communication and transparency that begins at the top

*It would be well worth the time, however long, to brainstorm on this most important question: "How do I make my business so much **FUN** that my employees can't wait to get to work?" My professional advice is to spend money on this one. You will get it back ten times over...at least!*

CHAPTER 13

USING YOUR STRENGTHS IN BUSINESS

In the early 1970's, I had taken a test and was absolutely devastated for two weeks once I was given the results. I walked around zombie-like for the longest time, head down to my knees.

My business partner and I had spent considerable funds from our business to acquire the use of an elaborate and detailed managerial questionnaire. It was designed to discover the management capabilities of our present and future managerial candidates. We were set on discovering whether they had the talents/skills prerequisite for high-level management. As owners, my partner and I decided also to take the test. We sent the finished exams off to the main offices in Minnesota and waited for the results. After two weeks, we received our answers – I was the only one in the company <u>not qualified</u> to be a manager.

Here I had worked so hard to be the best manager in the business, and I thought I was making significant progress.

Now I discovered I shouldn't have even tried as I was not that suited for this role. Needless to say, it was a major blow to my ego!

What I hadn't recognized at the time is that I was already using my skills and strengths creating a successful business. I did not understand that technical skills and innate strengths were two entirely different countries. I had moved from being the visionary entrepreneur to managing large numbers of people and managers.

This might be a good time to take a break and read Chapter 2, "The Entrepreneur, The Manager and The Technician," of the book *The E-Myth* written by Michael Gerber.

After getting over my disillusionment, I started using one of my innate strengths without even being conscious of what I was doing. One of my five main strengths is that of being a "connector": bringing individuals/groups together into a network of relationship.

Every Wednesday, we would bring all our store managers together at our office for two hours. The first hour was spent going over problems and how best to solve them. The second hour was a typical sales meeting: how to bring in new customers and to take better care of our existing customer base.

With this new knowledge that I was really not the manager-type, I simply gave out assignments to each manager: "At the next meeting, I would like each of you to give a presentation on inspiring your employees to greater productivity." Within a short six months, the managers were running all the meetings. All I had done was be clear about my real strengths, and step out of the way while creating an opportunity for them to come together each week and share their ideas.

Several years later, I read a management book by Peter Drucker, the management guru of the last century, entitled *The Effective Executive*. I will never forget the story at the beginning of Chapter 4, "Understaffing from Strength." Here is a bit of this story.

General Grant's appointment was a turning point for the Civil War. Up until that time, for three long years, the North had made no headway. Before Lincoln selected Grant, he had appointed, in succession, generals whose only common trait and primary qualification was their lack of any major weaknesses. Grant, on the other hand, had a major weakness, which was his love of drinking, but his major strength was that he could plan and win battles. It was a tough lesson to learn for President Lincoln, but one from which we all can learn.

In my own experience, I discovered if I spent $1,000 on a manager to correct a weakness, I might possibly get a return of $1,000 or less. However, if I invested $1,000 on a manager's strengths, I could be assured of a ten-fold return. The challenge is that the process in identifying those strengths in each and every person is uniquely different.

Most large corporations don't have the time or the resources to identify their employees' strengths. However, you do, and it is imperative that you give yourself this gift. Take some time and energy to inquire of friends and family what they perceive to be your greatest innate strengths. Think back to the time when you were four, five and six years of age, remembering incidents when those natural abilities of yours were obvious. What activities gave you the most energy? What gave you the most enjoyment? This will all assist you in discovering your innate talents.

My life became much easier when I spent some time with this exercise. No more trying to be something I'm not, or trying to be what my parents thought I should be. Here are my results: my five major strengths.

Connector: Bringing people together. When I was just five years of age, I remember I was the one always rounding up the neighborhood kids to play the games. All through high school and college, I was the individual bringing groups together to do FUN projects.

Playfulness: Bringing fun into every activity. I did it all throughout my growing-up years, and when I created a business, this was my main focus ~ FUN.

Idea Generation: When I was young, I was always creating ideas with others for some new game, some new activity. Later in life, I was inevitably the one creating new business ideas, starting brainstorming groups.

Enthusiasm: In my youth, I was always the one excited about any new idea or any work I was involved in. This was innate in my very nature ~ to be enthusiastic about life, about ideas, projects and people.

Optimism: I have always had a positive mental attitude. In the core of my being, I believe there is a resolution to every problem. This has been a major theme throughout my entire life demonstrated through multiple scenarios, personal and professional.

Albert Schweitzer was fond of saying, *"When you are using your talents to fill the needs of the world, you are doing what God wants."* My version is this, *"If you are using your strengths to fill the needs of your neighbor, you will be in harmony."*

I began asking potential employees in the interview process, "What are your strengths or talents, innate abilities vs. learned skills?" Only one out of a hundred seemed to have any idea of what I was speaking about.

We have a long way to go in this arena if we are to be effective in our lives and in our businesses. Those exploring this arena and putting it to good use will be the future leaders in the marketplace.

CHAPTER 14

HIRING THE BEST EMPLOYEES FOR YOUR BUSINESS

Why is hiring your <u>first employee</u> the most important skill to learn? Because this individual will have the potential to make or cost you money, and if you do not take the time and energy to master this ability, it could potentially cost your business a great deal.

When I am involved in a new creative business idea and working sixty to seventy hours every week to get it off the ground, I don't have the time it takes to manage the 1,001 details that go with it ~ advertising, taking phone calls or resumes, scheduling interviews and meeting with dozens of prospects. Sometimes I can get lucky, but the odds are like winning the lottery. And while there are very expensive programs and techniques in which you can invest a great deal of monies in order to find the right employee, the following is the best of the tried-and-tested during my many scenarios where finding a great match turned into a working relationship that went on for many years, and sometimes, for the duration of the business.

First, let's take a look at companies like Nordstrom, Microsoft and Disney. They each receive 1000's of resumes for each position. When I started out, I would get two, maybe three applicants for any one position I was trying to fill. These are not very good odds. Why are a hundred applicants going to be better than three? The answer is obvious: the more choices you have, the better the odds in finding the right person for the job. And I can just hear some of you entrepreneurs, "But I don't have time to interview 100 people!" My answer: You don't have the luxury not to do so!

Let's take this from a gambling game to an 80–90% sure thing by using some of the techniques I've learned over the past fifty years as an entrepreneur.

Here are five questions to be answered:

1. Be specific ~ What is the ideal employee for my kind of business/company?

2. How do I get a large number of prospects to apply?

3. How do I interview all these applicants with my limited time?

4. What kinds of questions should I be asking every applicant?

5. How do I finally select the one I am looking for to achieve a great match?

1. Be Specific: Profile Your Ideal Employee/ Associate.

Write down the ten values or characteristics and skills you want this person to have. Ask for the moon as you have nothing to lose at this point.

Example: Self-motivated, high integrity, energetic, optimistic, adventurous, enthusiastic, fun-loving, people-person, loves travel, likes new challenges…I almost forgot the most important one which I look for every time, "Must be teachable." On the skill level, the following description also determines how much you are willing to pay: Product knowledge, equipment knowledge, bookkeeping, computer skills, and years of experience. The more specific you are in your description, the greater your chances of attracting the ideal employee for any position.

2. How Do I Get a Large Number of Prospects to Apply?

Before the Internet, I always placed the largest ad I could barely afford in the Sunday edition of the

most-read newspaper in the area. It's still not a
bad idea as all large news journals are now on the
Internet. Signs such as "**Interviewing at Your Place
of Business**" are good. I never use the word "hiring"
for reasons I will later explain. Craigslist and all other
Internet job boards and recruiters are valuable.

Whenever I opened a restaurant, my goal was to
have 500 show up for interviews, whatever the cost.
I would hire from forty to seventy employees from
that number, depending on the store requirement.
Three months later, we were lucky if half of those
new hires were still with us. We still beat the national
average for turnovers by 50%. After that experience,
whenever we needed new employees, we would
strive to interview 50–100 in order to hire two, and
then would hope that both would work out. Sound
overwhelming? It can be if you don't put some of the
techniques to work in the following question, No. 3.
In order to get the maximum number of prospects
to show up, I would use the following terms: *"A
FUN place to work"; "Part of a growing team";
"Opportunity to learn the business"; "Bonuses
and rewards for outstanding work"; "Appearance
counts."*

We also listed benefits, but the thing that
always outweighed benefits was the need to be

acknowledged. In some establishments, I was hiring over 75 employees at one time, but I have used the same rules and techniques whether I have been hiring one employee or 1,000.

3. How do I Interview All These Applicants?

In 1981, I was hired to interview and secure a publicity director for a large shopping center in my area. I interviewed the shop owners in the mall to build a profile of the kind of person they wanted, wrote an ad based on their input, and had some 200 people show up for interviews. I hired two people to assist me and we had two days of interviews that lasted no more than five minutes, and sometimes only two minutes each. From this list, we selected ten finalists and on the third day, with thirty and sixty-minute screenings, we found our ideal candidate. By spending time and resources to accomplish this task, the shopping center acquired a director far above its expectations.

Rules for Interviewing:

Never answer the question for the applicant.

Never ask a question that can be answered "Yes" or "No."

Always be asking yourself whether this person fits the profile.

Always be evaluating this person on a scale of 1–5.

Be sensitive to body language and signs that imply/indicate addiction.

Be checking appearance as this will be the best they will look during their employment.

Give a questionnaire that you have prepared for them to fill out before the personal interview in order to make the best use of your time. On one sheet, create a self-inventory list. Have the applicant rate him/herself on a scale of 1–5, with 1 being the least. In your questions, use the following words: caring, honest, integrity, sensitive, enthusiastic, calm, high-energy, aware, stable, confident, can make quality decisions, healthy sense of humor, teachable, creative, enjoys working with a team, initiative, able to work independently, works well under pressure, stays rational in crisis, organized, outgoing, like yourself, and playful.

Have each applicant select the five words that best describe him or her. On a separate sheet, list all the technical skills, processes, and qualifications needed to do this job. Have one column for "no experience" and five columns from 1–5 headed with "minimally," "proficient," and "excellent." This will save you valuable time during your interview.

4. What are the best kinds of Questions?

Always ask open-ended questions. Here are some examples that will give your applicants the opportunity to tell you more of who they are, and what they bring to the table:

1. How did you decide on this kind of work?

2. Of all your past jobs, which one did you like the best? Why? Least? Why?

3. Why do you think I should hire you?

4. What strengths do you bring to this position? Be specific.

5. What are your career goals for the next two years? Five years?

6. If you could have made two improvements in your last job, what would they have been?

7. What are your plans for self-improvement?

8. What is it in your life that gets you really excited? Your passion?

9. What are the most important elements for you in your job? Why?

10. How often were you absent or late at your last job?

11. Describe for me the amount of supervision you prefer?

12. Who was your best employer? Your worst? Why?

13. Tell me three of your life goals.

These are just a few examples. Your particular business may require that you add or shorten this list. I find that the applicant during the process of answering these questions will talk him/herself into the job, or in other cases, out of the job. Of course, as the employer, throughout the interview, I am also asking myself the question whether I would enjoy being with this person? Would I trust him/her with my home, my customers, or my wallet?

At the end of the interview, I suggest we see whether the applicant likes working with us, and if we would like working with him/her. A trial period of one week, or in some cases, one month, is generally enough time to decide whether this will be a long-term hire. This gives each of us an out during this trial period. It is the same wisdom one uses in dating before committing to a long-term relationship.

5. How do I Make a Final Selection?

Through the past fifty years of selecting employees, and doing it currently with a new company, I have discovered it is not really that complicated if you have invested the time and energy to go through the first four questions. After the trial period, they will have selected you, and you them, and you will discover that it occurred more or less organically.

Now, that wasn't so hard, was it?!

With practice, trial and error, and using these techniques, you will find yourself improving rapidly at recruiting and hiring. The first four managers I hired didn't work out. I was in a position of needing to learn how to hire with more skill, or my business would never have been able to grow. For many years now, I've considered myself proficient 90% of the time, and in today's market, that tends to be a high rate of success. With practice, you, too, will recruit and hire with great skill finding those exceptional matches that will make your business thrive!

CHAPTER 15

LEARNING THE ART
OF DELEGATION

How does one go from working 100 hours a week to three hours a week? It only took me twelve years to learn this one! Hopefully, you can do it in a much shorter period of time if you can take in the information in this chapter. If your goal is to have more free time and to have fun with your family, I guarantee you this will work!

When I had thirty-six employees, as we did at our first Farrell's, we had to delegate all the small jobs at the outset: cashier, busboy, waiter, cook, dishwasher and fountain person. The more difficult positions were the supervisor or lead person in these areas, with the most challenging position being the store manager. If you don't get that position right, the whole operation will fail.

The first step is hiring the most qualified person for this position, as you learned about in the previous chapter. The next step is like jumping off a cliff and trusting that you will land safely because you are giving your creation over to someone else to manage. You trust and give specific guidelines for the person to succeed. At this juncture, and if you are a wise business owner, you are giving up a certain amount of control and the dysfunction of micro-management, hoping that your newly hired manager will take the baton and run with it.

I view delegation as a sort of art form because it requires a great deal of skill, knowledge and timing. <u>Skill</u> through trial and error, and a great deal of practice in knowing what to say and how to say it; <u>Knowledge</u> of the other person's strengths and weaknesses and temperament; and <u>Timing</u> in knowing when to give out an assignment or directive, and knowing how and when to monitor completion.

My biggest problem has not been so much with skill, knowledge, or timing, but rather how to "delegate" in the first place. "I can do it all myself" was my main mantra, and the rest of these mantras fell in line right behind it:

I can do it better than anyone else.

I need to have lots of things to do in order to feel important.

I need to solve everyone else's problems in order to have job security.

The more problems I have, the more I am needed.

Do these ring true with anyone you know? Perhaps yourself? If so, know that you have lots of company in the marketplace!

Sure, I needed to develop the skill, knowledge and timing, but how could I learn these attributes when I don't delegate in the first place? I had 50–100 items on my "To Do" list every single day. Then in 1970 came a business best seller *Up The Organization* by Robert Townsend, the guy who made AVIS number two in the car rental business.

On page 46 of Townsend's book, there is a chapter on "Delegation of Authority." This book was what got me started on delegation. Then in 1973, I went to a two-day seminar based solely on the recognition of my habits of allowing my workers to pile on notes, memos, assignments, until I became bogged down and virtually ineffective in my work day.

I believe that seminar was called **"Get the Monkeys Off Your Back!"** I had no idea the number of monkeys I was carrying around until I put what I learned to good use. I was great at saying "Yes" every time someone asked whether I could handle a problem. What I began to learn was that the best person able to solve the problem was the one giving it to me in the first place.

I gave that person the trust and authority to see whether he could solve it and if he was not able to do so, I suggested he come back in a day or a week, and we would explore other options.

It seems initially I had set up a scenario as the boss that they could, and should, come to me with any problem. The error in this mindset was that while this structure met the need in me to feel valued and important, my employees/managers remained stuck without learning how to come up with their own creative solutions.

I started looking at every piece of paper given to me from the perspective that each one was one more monkey on my back, and by the end of the day, I might have twenty to twenty-five added to what I had started with that morning. I made a 3x5 card with the words "<u>Delegate First</u>" and put it on my bathroom mirror so that every morning when I went to shave, this was my reminder to delegate throughout the day's activities.

My reality of being overwhelmed with work took a surprising turn even within a few months. My workers began to act like adults as they took on more and more responsibility. It became an adult/adult relationship rather than a boss/employee interaction. The amazing thing was that as they grew, I grew as well, and the business began to thrive more than ever.

Before this, I was unaware of how my bad habit of doing everything myself instead of delegating was stifling the growth of our business. I had been the very bottle-neck that was slowing down our progress in the marketplace. I was unable to get out of the way with a ton of monkeys being carried on my back.

My first thought on the way to work became, to whom can I delegate the items on my list today? Now, with practice, you can develop the skill, knowledge and timing to be a master of delegation.

You can take courses on the art of delegation, but nothing will give you more information than doing it on a daily basis. <u>Delegate ~ Delegate ~ Delegate ~ Delegate FIRST! Do It Now!</u>

Incidentally, when I opened Yonny Yonson's Soup, Salad, Sandwich & Yogurt restaurants in 1977, after hiring the manager, I told her I would be leaving on a vacation with my wife to Tahiti where there would be no phones and no way to reach me. I had graduated to a new level of delegation!

We opened March 3rd, and I left for two weeks on April 4th. This delegation worked so well that this person was still managing the store after sixteen years. Within three years, I was working three hours a week with five stores in operation. Each of my managers had full responsibility to operate his or her store, hiring, firing and managing the payroll for fifteen employees each.

And what was I doing in the meantime? Business consulting, giving speeches, leading seminars and writing— all things I love to do!

We will be learning more about what keeps all of this in order. It is the same thing that keeps our solar system in order... ALIGNMENT, explained further in Chapter 17.

CHAPTER 16

BECOMING MORE CREATIVE: MOVING FROM THE COMPETITIVE MIND TO THE CREATIVE MIND

I titled this chapter **"Becoming More Creative."** Another appropriate title could have been **"Remembering to be Creative."**

What happens to that creative spark in us between the ages of five to seven years? I believe "what happens to us" is our 100-year old, industrial-age educational system.

The question then becomes, "What on earth do we do about it?" I would like to propose that one major step would be to identify and move from competition to cooperation, or better yet, to move from the competitive mind to the creative mind?

I remember a time some years back when I was playing tennis with my good buddy, Jeffry W. Meyers, and I was not having much fun. You see, Jeffry was being extremely competitive on that hot summer day at the Newport High School tennis courts, and I wasn't having much fun because I was winning all the games too easily. The score was something like 5-love in my favor. I stopped mid-game, called Jeffry over to the net, and suggested a new and different approach. "You are trying to beat me, and it is not working." I then suggested, "Why not try moving from the 'competitive mind' to the 'creative mind'. Play the most creative tennis you can possibly imagine, and leave beating me out of the picture." Jeffry won the next five games, until the set score was five games to five.

He had moved into the "zone." What a difference! I can't recall who won the set, but I do remember how much fun it was playing creative tennis!

In my past business life, whenever I began to dwell singularly on "market share," what the competition was doing, and how I could beat them, it required so much energy and thought that I would become exhausted. I discovered if I put that same energy to work on how I could creatively improve my business, improving over last year's figures, it always worked in my favor. My theory is if I try to beat the competition, I end up defeating myself just like my friend was defeating himself in our tennis match.

Moving from the competitive mind to the creative mind requires a conscious effort. The way most of us were trained from childhood and in our schools is that we need to compete to get ahead in life, period.

The most creative individuals I know do not have competition as their primary focus, being better than anyone else. Rather, they are intensely focused on improving their own personal excellence in their passionate projects.

Just as there is a more powerful way to think, there is also a more powerful way to act. We can all make the decision to think and act more creatively in our daily affairs.

Here are my five steps to becoming more creative in life.

1. Be in the process of learning to be open to any and all ideas that come your way.

In 1974, I wrote this affirmation to help open my mind to unlimited possibilities. "I am accomplishing my life goals by soaking up ideas and learning like a sponge." Another: "I am becoming such an enthusiastic sponge, people are exposing me to all they know." And: "I am now learning how to ask probing open-ended questions so I receive complete answers to all I need."

2. Be in the process of learning to love problems/challenges.

The first time I heard this, I thought it was definitely a dumb idea. Whenever I would talk to Charlie Tremendous Jones either on the phone or in person, the first thing out of his mouth was, "Do you have any problems?" Of course, I always had a major problem I was facing because that is the nature of being in business. I would tell him my number one problem, and he would say, "That's great! You can't grow if you don't have problems, and the bigger, the better!"

I finally caught on to what he was saying and realized that we are all born problem solvers. We have been doing this since the beginning of time. In business, we have a tremendous opportunity for personal growth. Why? Because each and every day we are confronted with 100's of problems. Now, instead of pushing them away, I welcome them with open arms. Well, at least much more so than in the past.

3. Be in the process of learning to become "childlike."

This, of course, is different than "childish." What I mean by "childlike" is this. A child is a good model to pattern your life after. He sees his life as a series of problems to be solved. From learning to get food, get changed, learning to walk, using his hands, climbing on the table to get that lamp… you get the picture. He goes about "problem solving" with inventive relish. We could consciously do the same. Our problems, of course, become more complex, with greater ramifications, like how to deal with an authoritarian, negative boss. This is what you have been in training for since birth. Problem solving is not peripheral to life. It is a key ingredient to the activity of living. As we get older, we seem to set our own limitations. Children don't have limits. Think like a child…become like a child. What did the great master say 2,000 years ago? "If you would inherit the kingdom, then you must become like a little child." No matter the arena of life, these are wise words.

4. Be in the process of learning to set goals, visualize and affirm what you desire.

I have discovered that the most creative individuals are involved in all three of these activities. They have a vision of what they are creating, they have set goals no matter how long it takes to reach their target, they affirm daily the realization of that goal in some way, and they are consistently taking action steps leading toward their desired end result.

In 1972, I went to my first self-help seminar. It lasted four days and one of the affirmations I came away with was this: "I am a highly creative person in all parts of my life, always becoming more and more open to God's Divine Plan." I repeated this five times per day for two full years until I could actually receive a compliment about something I had created without shrugging it off. Then I would hear myself saying, "Thank you very much." In the past, I would say, "Oh, it really was no big deal…", and in the process, not only degrading myself, but the individual who had just given me the compliment.

5. Be in the process of learning to do it now!

I would say most of us are masters of procrastination. I was, and to such a degree that even before I made a phone call, I would sit by the phone mentally thinking of what I was going to say, sometimes even for ten to fifteen minutes.

This was always the case when calling someone I didn't know. Then came another ten to fifteen minutes mental exercise going over what the person on the other end of the line might say. By the time I had finally gotten up the courage to make the call, my stomach was in knots. I had so effectively postponed stepping into the action step giving ample time for fear to set in. When I made the call without giving it too much thought, stepping into the energy of the moment, there wasn't time to think of all the mistakes I could possibly make in the process.

Shortly thereafter, I made a sign posting it right on the front of my phone that said: "Do it Now!" I committed to saying this mantra to myself, "Do it Now!" some fifty times per day until I moved into a place of easily doing things now vs. putting things off. It's very difficult to be creative when stuck in procrastination using up valuable energy that can be put to a more powerful use.

These are some of the ideas I have used to remember to stay in the creative mind.

A very creative friend of ours, Karen Dedrickson, came up with this in one of the Business Round Tables I was facilitating: "I am always (my word) unlearning mis-information about myself." Karen is a most creative artisan. Right after she had made this statement, she came up with another gem addressing old habits that can keep us from expressing our individual creativity: "Cracking open the hard nut of habit releases the juicy oils of opportunity."

Fortunately, I had a pen and paper handy so I could record that one!

I have no doubt the primary reason I am now daily surrounded by creative individuals is because I am acknowledging the creativity in myself more.

It is commensurate with the truth that you can never see, nurture, or protect fully what is in another unless/until you can see, nurture and protect fully that same thing within yourself. It is most wise to avoid individuals who will not protect those vulnerable and creative parts of yourself that are struggling to find the light of day. I am also finding now that as I am actively protecting and nurturing more of what is vulnerable and creative within myself, others on similar creative paths find it more fun to be around me.

What are those items that keep you actively immersed in the creative mind? I suggest you take a few moments right now and list at least five of them, and more if you can. Do it here. It's okay to mark up this book. Sometimes all we need is permission to be creative. Go ahead! Tear out some magazine pages, and build your own storyboard, or a treasure map. My favorite business books are well worn and well marked. This shows the love I have had for their content!

My hope is that you love this book enough to mark it up! This is a good sign that your competitive mind is well on its way toward becoming a creative mind!

CHAPTER 17

CREATING ALIGNMENT

My first consulting job was with Washington Aircraft, a company owned by my good friend, Stan. I had been used to having my own businesses run pretty smoothly because we always had a common vision or goal. What made it fun was that all the employees were in alignment with the same goal, or, if not, it became so uncomfortable for them that they would eventually quit.

When I began working with Stan's business, it became apparent that they were definitely not all on the same page. Having alignment was essential as the twelve technicians were installing new avionics in existing private airplanes where safety is a major concern.

Stan and I began a series of weekly meetings with all the workers. On the third week, I decided to give the alignment exercise. This was designed to find out how many in this group were aligned with the goals of the company. But first, we had agreed on a target or goal. After that, I had them place arrows in the alignment model.

Following is an example of how this works.

Creating Alignment

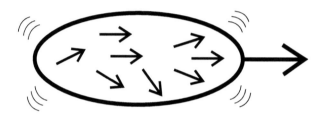

This model represents some movement, but is sporadic and jerky.

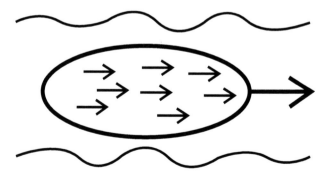

This model represents incredible movement toward the mission or goal.

<u>Agreement</u> can be superficial and manufactured in outward appearance. It can be manipulated by a paycheck, tenure benefits, etc. Even so, there usually will be some movement toward the goal.

<u>Alignment</u> is not agreement. It is the experience when individuals of a team have chosen to support the team goal, and also feel that the team goal/vision supports them in their individual goals and values. With alignment, there is far greater freedom for disagreement, debate and argument, because underlying all discussions regarding process or the "how-to" is a common mission or common purpose that creates an energy of common focus. The result will be superior due to the constructive environment created by a range of ideas and input.

Here is what transpired in their process.

Each individual had a copy of the circle with the outer arrow symbolizing the company vision, and the inside area of the circle being empty. They were to draw their individual arrow in the mix signifying where they felt their energy was in relationship to the company vision represented by the outer arrow. The next step was they drew in everyone else's arrow according to their own personal perceptions. Their sheets were turned in anonymously. I then compiled a final model using the data from all the sheets. This was the final outcome.

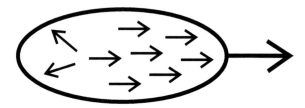

As you can see, there is some divergence here. There are two arrows going against the flow causing resistance in the movement of the company. Within two weeks, two people quit the company. They and everyone else knew the reason, and not a word was spoken. Stan, the owner said, "That was easy. I didn't even have to go through the trauma of letting them go!" As you know, it only takes one to slow down the energy of the whole team in a business that is attempting to be productive.

And what was the goal they were striving for? To be 100% productive 80% of the time. At an earlier meeting, they had agreed their productivity was in the range of 20-40%. I then wanted to make their goal intensely visual.

On a 30-foot long sheet of butcher paper, I had printed in large letters, "This company is 100% productive at least 80% of the time." We then had the banner hung high in the hanger where they worked so that every day the workers could see a visual reminder of this goal. It was like a billboard staring them in the face where they worked.

I liken the alignment model to a piece of Romax electrical wire that is used in the construction of every home. When there is any piece of resistance in that wire, you do not receive the full amount of energy to the outlet, and sometimes it can result in permanent damage to the appliance that is plugged in at that spot.

Every business, to run smoothly and at peak effectiveness, needs to have all its human resources working together for a common purpose. If your workers are there only for a paycheck and retirement benefits, most likely you will have many arrows pointing backwards, and the fun has gone out of their reasons for showing up at work each day.

While this model will work for families, sports teams, non-profit organizations, and government entities, it is absolutely essential if you wish to succeed in business. I have now used this 100's of times, and it is always an eye opener and a confirmation of what you expect is going on in the organization.

The major benefit of going through this exercise is that everyone on your company team will know whether or not you are succeeding to your full potential and why that is the case. Once you have a number of people working together toward a common outcome or goal, the most important exercise you can do is checking in with this alignment model.

In Peter Senge's book *The Fifth Discipline*, in the chapter on "Team Learning," he makes the case for alignment by using two examples of groups working together to achieve extraordinary results. One was the Boston Celtics with eleven world championships in thirteen years, and the other, jazz musicians who end up "playing in the groove" when an ensemble "plays as one." Although they can feel it at the time, it is very hard to explain to others so they might use words and phrases such as "magical," "time stood still," "it was all in slow motion," "it flowed through you rather than from you," and "time flew by."

This has happened to me many times when I was giving a talk or speech to a group of people. The audience and I were in perfect alignment, and in an unexpected moment, ideas and thoughts came out of my mouth that seemed to come from somewhere else. I have sometimes remarked, "Did you hear what I just said?" as if it didn't come from me, but there was an awareness that it was needed to be said at that time and place. The conditions were right.

Some of our most creative right-brain moments happen out of the blue. This can only be explained as energy or electricity moving in alignment with what we are doing at the time. For greater insight on this subject, I suggest you read the first three pages of the above-mentioned chapter.

If you need more proof for the power of alignment working all around us, look to nature, the planets and the universe, and you will experience our greatest teacher in action.

SECTION THREE

HOW TO
NURTURE YOURSELF

While Growing Your Business

CHAPTER 18

MAKING MIS-TAKES

Have you ever worried about making the right decision? Well, in my opinion, there are no right or wrong decisions. There are only decisions. Better yet, let's call them "wise" and "unwise" decisions. That way we will only know much later on whether or not they were what most of us call, a "good decision."

Un-decision, or indecision, causes a great deal of stress and loss of energy. Many years ago, I heard this phrase: "Make a decision, make a decision, make a decision, and then make it right!" Worrying about making the "right" decision will drive you nuts. At least, that has been something of what I have been learning throughout my own life.

This chapter is about making decisions that didn't work out, and were considered unwise as time went by. Mis-takes are learning glitches that we need for our growth in a chosen field of work. Without my own glitches, setbacks and mis-takes, I would not have had the expertise to move on, let alone the wisdom to write this book.

Another analogy I like to use with mis-takes is this. In making movies, there is the terminology of "takes" used when actors are doing several redo's of the same scene.

I've never heard of a feature movie, or a director for that matter, winning an Academy Award for creating a movie on the first take! That means that every single scene would be perfect on the first take! In fact, the reality is that several takes are used for each scene, with some actors and/or directors insisting on this because often things improve. And look at all the laughter we've had through the years from "outtakes," "bloopers"…those mis-takes made during scenes.

Life is like that, including life in business and the marketplace. Can you imagine some mythical director in the marketplace holding up the "take board" and after you've made one mis-take in your business, he yells, "No more… that's it!" Well, some treat themselves with as much leniency. Give yourselves a break! Begin to look at every mis-take as one more chance to "improve the scene" ~ learn a little more, get some more wisdom under your belt, fine tune your expertise in a certain area.

Here are a number of mis-takes I have made through the years, and what I am continuing to learn from them. And it should be noted, there have been plenty of "outtakes" that have kept my colleagues and me laughing for years!

1. Hiring seasoned musicians with bad habits during my nightclub days.

These guys were used to playing three numbers and then having a break. It was costing me money as people would get up and leave during the breaks. What I needed was forty-five minutes of non-stop music, so in addition to hiring people with fewer bad habits, I decided to join the band as the leader and played the drums, and I didn't stop for six years! We started playing four forty-five minute sets each evening. So, for the next six years, everything worked great!

2. Hiring a policeman to be our doorman, and ID checker.

This was a disaster! After some of the patrons had downed a few drinks, they wanted to take on the "man in uniform." One night, our doorman cop had his shirt almost torn off. After two years of problems, we finally trained and

Becoming A Creative Entrepreneur

hired our own bouncer/doorman with great success. No more trouble. It seems some folks needed to taunt authority figures just for the hell of it!

3. Opening Elroy's Ice Cream Parlour across the street from The Blue Banjo in Pioneer Square.

This became a losing proposition. We didn't get a lot of families coming down to a nightlife area like Pioneer Square, and of course, Elroy's was designed for families. Over a three-year period, we calculated our losses at $10,000, which was a lot of money in 1963! I eventually called this my experiment with fancy ice cream dishes.

On the other hand, without opening Elroy's, I probably would never have met Bob Farrell and eventually opened the Farrell's in Bellevue, WA, which became the first territorial franchise. My partner, Joe Rutten, and I called Elroy's our $10,000 wind tunnel; appropriate since we had both worked for Boeing. This experiment also gave us the confidence we needed to take the future necessary risks on an idea that had not yet been proven: selling ice cream sundaes and food in regional shopping centers.

180

4. Hiring professional waiters to staff our Farrell's restaurants.

This was another disaster! The professional waiters were coming in with too many bad habits and definitely not what our store needed. We needed young college kids with lots of energy to make it work. Within months, we figured this out and made excellent hires. The ones with high grade-point averages seemed to work out best; they had already made wise use of their time. None of them became professional waiters, but we made good use of their skills for four years and we did, in fact, put a considerable number of these young men and women through college.

5. Perhaps our biggest mistake was opening a Farrell's Ice Cream Parlour in Vancouver, BC.

We had secured a Canadian partner to go into business with us, but when he backed out, we decided to go forward with the idea anyway. This became very difficult as we had to deal with a range of Canadian customs and laws that were totally unfamiliar to us. The first year, we lost $80,000, and by the time we sold the restaurant, we were only losing $20,000 per year. I was driving up from Seattle to Vancouver and back every week to promote and market this business just so we could cut our weekly losses in order to sell. This took twenty months, almost two years, to accomplish. What did I learn? Do not open a business that is not in your country or market area unless you have a vested partner in the business who is also a native to that region, living near the establishment, and familiar with all business regulations and requirements connected to that city/county/state/country.

6. After creating The Breadline Restaurant & Soup Kitchen, I sold the operating store and the concept, assuming that the new owners would not change the original.

In fact, this is exactly what they did in hopes of making greater profit. Not only did the buyers lose a vast amount of money on the second store built, but the original store lasted only four years because they were allowing the quality to diminish without check. These were absentee owners and they were operating from Hawaii; definitely not a formula for success. Shortly thereafter, I read the story of Walt Disney and how he had done the same thing. Learning his lesson, from that time forward, Disney would only sell copies of what he created, and that is exactly what I did next time around.

When I created Yonny Yonson's Restaurants, I decided to keep the concept. While I did sell a couple of copies, this creation supported me for nearly twenty years.

7. In 1975, along with a partner, I bought the Merchant's Café, the oldest restaurant establishment in Seattle, WA.

The purpose was to make a few changes and build up the clientele. We bought this business in order to make money, and for reasons I learned later on in life, this formula never works for me. I am great at creating an establishment from scratch, from the ground up. However the range of skills required for profitable management are just not my forte. I usually fall flat on my face whenever I do something just for the purpose of making money. When it's my idea, or if I am totally involved creatively in building the business from the ground up, I am 80–90% successful. When it is an existing business or not my idea, my chances of succeeding dwindles to about 10–20%. This propensity was proven in two later ventures. After three years, we sold the Merchant's Café at a loss.

Mistakes will happen, and the theme of this chapter is to remember that every mis-take is only a stepping-stone in moving to your next level of expertise and wisdom. In business, if we had never tried anything new due to fear of failure, we would never have acquired the knowledge and wisdom that proved essential in our future successes. Studying and reading about business practices alone will not give one the confidence required to be an expert over time. What is essential is on the job, day-to-day running and operating of your own business. This will give you the building blocks to become proficient as you and your business passionately make their mark in the marketplace.

In the book *Outliers*, author Malcolm Gladwell offers a compelling case for putting in "your 10,000 hours" of practice to become a high-level performer. And I would concur wholeheartedly. You cannot improve on the activity of opening and running your own business, for 10,000 hours or more, in providing the practice one needs to excel in the marketplace.

When my partner, Joe and I, opened our first Farrell's Ice Cream Parlour, we each put in a minimum of 4,000 hours the first year. That was a fast learning curve as we had thirty-six employees to train and manage. We made dozens of mistakes that first year, but remember, we were just practicing! What was holding our feet to the fire was the keen awareness that if we did not learn from our mistakes quickly, we would be out of business in six to twelve months, a stark reality for some 80% of businesses each year.

I always try to remember that mistakes are the most powerful learning tools we have. Always perceive them as blessings for your personal growth. There is no quicker way of learning who you are than being in the marketplace and being in personal relationships. Creating and operating your own business will definitely serve in putting you on a fast track to personal growth!

CHAPTER 19

VISION CIRCLES

In Chapter 2, we discussed the elements required in building your vision. It is of the utmost importance to create a support group for nurturing yourself and your vision. This is a group of individuals who share a common bond, sharing similar interests or a mutual desire to grow. This can be a group of three to six individuals who meet on a regular basis each month, or preferably, once every week. The purpose here is to focus on living your dreams rather than on what is not working. This is not a time and place where you give advice, but rather where you support and see each other creating what you are focusing on in your lives.

In 1989, after many attempts at creating Master Mind Groups, using the Master Mind principles, my wife, Jane, and I created a simple model/tool for continued on-going group facilitation. We discovered this was a powerful way to support others and vice-versa. When running your own business, it is wise to share what is going on with your business with a few fellow entrepreneurs who need and wish to give support. The ideas laid down in our Vision Circle booklet are simple and easy to use.

We have reprinted the book below for your convenience.

Booklet Published, Copyright 1989, for use in Business Development Seminars.

Co-Author/Editor: Jane Bakken/Co-Founder, Owner of

Northwest Institute of Excellence,
Business Consulting Firm

VISION CIRCLES

A Powerful Tool in
Creating What you Want

"Vision Circles" is just one valuable process in facilitating the creation of what you want…easily and effortlessly. Use it as a tool while being open to other processes.

In creating what you want, it is important to know where you are ~ **current reality** ~ as well as what you want ~ **vision/goal**. If you actually are in Chicago wanting to travel to New York...yet **you think** you are in Seattle, well, you will end up in deep waters...literally!

Consequently, the first part of "**Vision Circles**" is designed to facilitate you in getting in touch with exactly where you are at in this moment. Practice describing current reality to yourself and others ~ an objective news report of what is going on in your life, as well as your feelings about that. This may seem obvious, however, often wasted energy is spent on **WHY you are where you are,** or **WHY something has happened** rather than investing that same energy into focusing on and creating what it is you want.

The other section is designed to clarify for you the "**want**" ~ **your goal/vision.**

Allow the following guidelines to make it easy for you... and have **FUN living your dreams!**

===

CURRENT REALITY:

1. Form a group of individuals with common bond, similar interests; even a mutual desire to grow is a great core beginning.

2. Each individual shares informally of the past week's events, results, action steps, completions, creations, etc. This is an objective report of what is happening in

your life and your feelings about that ~ not an analysis of WHY or an attempt to advise someone else what to do.

NOTE: Each individual in the group fully acknowledges the person speaking. The individual sharing is also developing his/her own ability to receive fully the acknowledgement from others as well as from her/himself.

NOTE: Getting in touch with "current reality" is very different from positive thinking. Whenever you suppress or repress negative feelings, your subconscious gets the idea that they are powerful, and in doing so, you actually give them more power. By acknowledging what is going on as well as your feelings about that, you can more freely make choices to take your next step.

===

VISION/GOAL:

1. Each individual describes three specific results he/ she wants this week in **vivid word pictures,** setting aside for now any recommendation or ideas on process, how-to's, methods, advice, etc.

Example: "This week, I want $3,000 in cash, easily and effortlessly, to see our investment property sold for $180,000 or better...and to create the $10,000 for our trip to Europe next month."

2. Every other individual in the group (time element providing) feeds back to the asking individual clear, specific word picture/vision of the three items actually seeing them realized.

Example: "John, I can see you with that $3,000 cash. You are just driving out of the bank after depositing the money. One of the ten prospective purchasers has just finalized the papers for your investment property selling for $180,000 or better…at terms even better than you were asking for! (and so on)

==

GUIDELINES:

1. Give very clear, specific, detailed word pictures.

2. Each individual is encouraged to hitchhike on the word pictures of another ~ build the energy and the life of the "visual."

3. Asking individual is encouraged to participate fully in receiving visuals of the group.

4. Visuals are free of investing in any one process, any certain action step, manipulation, advice, etc.

5. Key is to **HAVE FUN** ~ let the four-year old in you come out and play!

6. Unconditional acceptance is important ~ an environment created where each individual can experience freedom to share new ideas and thoughts as well as thoughts and feelings about current situations.

7. Support does not include giving of advice.

8. State your wants simply without manipulating other people or circumstances.

9. Practice releasing any investment in the process ~ "how" it is going to come about. As soon as you become invested in a certain process or processes, it is possible to block what you really want coming to you simply because you cannot see the HOW. There are an infinite number of ways for any dream to become a reality. By limiting the HOW, you can create unnecessary delays, or create the result with far more difficulty and struggle.

Therefore, let go of the process ~ allow the vision to dictate the **HOW**…thereby allowing the results to come to you in the easiest, fastest way possible…with an unlimited number of possibilities!

Example: (less effective in that you are choosing for someone else)

"I want my ex to pay me the $3,000 he/she owes me."

(more effective)

"I want $3,000 or more…in the fastest way possible, from any source."

Example: (less effective ~ choosing for someone else)

"I want Cheryl to marry me."

(more effective)

"I want to marry Cheryl…or better, and create a marriage that is exciting, fulfilling, spontaneous, fun, adventurous…"

LIVE YOUR VISION….NOW!
(End of Booklet)

==

Try this out for a month and see how it works for you. And remember, these guidelines are not etched in stone. Feel free to be creative and adjust the Vision Circle guidelines to suit your particular needs or that of your group.

I cannot emphasize enough how important it is to have an ongoing support group, individuals who are there to support you rather than always protect or to give you advice. That is why family members are often not the best candidates for your Vision Circle, at least not the first one. I would have given anything to have had a wise support group when I was opening my first business after leaving my engineering job at The Boeing Company.

Do whatever it takes to create this for yourself. You deserve it!

CHAPTER 20

CELEBRATING YOUR 100TH BIRTHDAY PARTY!

Most of us don't get a second chance at life…or, do we?

One morning in 1888, Alfred awoke to a newspaper article written by a French reporter that gave him the chills. There in black and white, on the front page of the obituary section, he was reading himself being described as the "Merchant of Death." In reality, his equally infamous brother had died suddenly, and the paper had switched their names in error. Alfred was the inventor of dynamite and had amassed a fortune from the manufacture and sale of explosives. He saw himself as a man who was making the world a better place by building roads and tunnels. To his dismay, he discovered that the world, at that time, perceived him much differently.

In response to this, Alfred Nobel spent the rest of his life rewriting his own personal history by developing the most valued of prizes given to those who have done the most for the cause of world peace. We are now familiar with the Nobel Peace Prize awarded in Norway on December 10th each year (the anniversary of Alfred Nobel). Fortunately, for the world, Alfred Nobel was given a second life.

<u>The same can be true for you.</u>

In 1972, I was asked this question by an individual whom I highly respected, "What do you want it to say on your tombstone?" In order to bring the question into the here and now, I adjusted the question to, "What DOES it say on my tombstone?" The question bothered me to such an extent that I decided to get up at 6:00 a.m. every morning, go to my office, sit at my desk with a cup of tea, and attempt to answer that exact question. After four months, on April 7th, I had finally arrived at an answer. It scared me to such a degree that I avoided telling anyone for six months.

This simple exercise literally changed my life. For the first time, I was now writing my own script. Until then, I had been living out dutifully the script written by my parents, my older sister and her husband, and others, and worse yet, I didn't even know it! I was actually living my life in a way that they thought was best for me, bless their hearts, and, of course, with my cooperation. I will now give you the secret to doing this exercise that I had once made so difficult.

YOU GET TO MAKE IT UP!

And you get to change it whenever you please. My epitaph has now evolved into a full-page story of my 100th birthday party, including who I am, my guests and what I am being acknowledged for in my life. Guess what? At least half of the goals I described over thirty years ago have come to pass. It is important to see it big as most of you will have ample time to accomplish whatever you come up with. What will emerge from this process, rising as cream to the surface, are your authentic passions and values in life.

In my small group seminars, once participants have established some degree of familiarity with each other, I ask them to make up, creating in detail, their 100th birthday party. Who are the guests attending? Where is the party located? What are you being acknowledged for by friends and family? I then give them one week, not four months, to come back and share their story.

The result of this exercise is encouraging. Most of the time, as a group, we are hearing how the world is a better place because of this one individual, his/her vision and contributions. We also hear of a number of Nobel Prize recipients. I remember one lady who had just turned seventy-five years of age, and she was beside herself with excitement. Before the class, she had been in a mode of preparing herself and her estate for her anticipated demise. This was more than just the systematic wise actions we all take at some point and then put in a drawer. Rather she was mentally preparing herself to die, soon, and she knew it. After the exercise of creating her 100th Birthday Party, she got so excited because she realized that she had a lot more living to do. She informed us, "I'm going to go right out and get my teeth fixed and start taking dancing lessons because now I have at least twenty-five more good years!"

Whether you live to be 100 or more doesn't really matter. What does seem to matter more than anything is to keep creating goals, living feeling the edge of creative tension, and primarily, having a goal to be full of health and enjoying life until your last breath.

I am always amazed by the energy in the room when someone is sharing his or her 100th birthday celebration. And what exactly does this have to do with business? Everything! For me, business is where I learn about life. It has been said that the two arenas where you have ample opportunity to learn the most while you are on this planet are in relationships and in the marketplace. I am convinced this is true. Focusing on my 100th birthday helps me stay present in these two arenas. A most unusual side benefit from doing this exercise is that it has given me tremendous freedom in all areas of my life.

I hope your 100th Birthday celebration is as exciting as mine!

Remember ~ Alfred Nobel made it up. So can you!

CHAPTER 21

SPIRITUALITY IN BUSINESS

How does the term "spirituality" fit in the business model?

Have you ever walked into a business and felt the "energy" of that business? It could be a retail store, an accounting firm, a service station, even a manufacturing plant. The atmosphere is charged with electricity, and you can feel it on some level. This energy I refer to as the "spirit" of that business.

It is the unseen element that you know is present bringing some new idea as a product or service out into the marketplace. Some refer to it as the "electricity," the energy of that idea. You can almost rate it on a scale of 1–10 with 10 being the most intense. Employees are "charged up" and they have a mission, a purpose to accomplish. The business has an expressed mission, vision, and core values, and all are on board and in alignment helping to make their goals a reality. Being part of a vision greater than themselves is important in bringing some meaning because this is a place/time where they are investing a large percentage of their day.

Please don't misunderstand. This has nothing to do with "religion." Generally, with institutional religion, there are many dogmas and rules. In business, it appears that the less power and control exerted over the employees, the more likely they will be filled up with enthusiasm for their jobs. That is what I refer to as "spirituality in business."

Take for example the retail chain of Nordstroms originating right here in my hometown of Seattle, Washington. Nordstroms to this day has one primary rule for every person it hires. It goes something like this: **Rule #1: "Use your good judgment in all situations. There will be no additional rules."** That's it! No wonder Nordstrom stores sustain such a high level of "spiritual energy."

And from the book, *A Whole New Mind ~ Moving From the Information Age to the Conceptual Age*, written by Daniel H. Pink, comes the statement, ***"Most business executives defined spirituality in much the same way ~ not a religion, but as 'a basic desire to find purpose and meaning in one's life.'*** An interview of some 100 CEO's led to the conclusion, ***"It was found that companies that acknowledged spiritual*** *values and aligned them with company goals outperformed those that did not."*

As stated in earlier chapters, I was more successful when I started a business from scratch rather than buying a business and trying to make it work with an already-existing philosophy, culture and employees. Whenever I start a business from the very beginning, I am the architect and have the opportunity to create the foundation for success at that time. Meaning and spiritual values are then deeply woven into that business for me.

My most successful opening was The Breadline Restaurant in 1974. In our one week of pre-opening training, I brought in an outside seminar leader to conduct a three-day workshop on how to realize your highest potential using your strengths and God-given talents to the maximum. All the employees realized they were totally responsible for their own individual success and became aligned with our goal to serve 1,000 people a day, easily and effortlessly. It was what I would call a "spiritual" event.

In your own business, it is your responsibility to be the designer of your business, the architect. Just like the owner of an ocean liner, everyone needs to be on board with the direction the boat is headed. I believe most businesses fail because the architect has created an unworkable design.

Look at what happened to the *Titanic*. To save money, the shipbuilders decided to design the ship without a double hull, a choice that cost many their lives. To be a "spiritual" enterprise in the marketplace, I would say that the safety and well-being of your employees and your customers needs to be your #1 priority, even before that of making a profit. If you put them first, there is an energy that will be infused in your business, and you will attract, eventually, all the customers you need.

Some bakeries, cookie stores, for example, have built into their design the aroma of freshly baked cookies being "blown out" onto the sidewalk. Customers pick up the delicious scent as they are walking by, and more often than not, go in and buy cookies. We're speaking of the same dynamics. By placing the well-being of your employees and your customers at the top of your list, this energy will be picked up in the marketplace, and you will attract more customers than you can possibly imagine!

Just the other day, a well-respected business professional mentioned to me that this is in fact his current barometer for determining which company he awards business to when all other variables are constant. If he discovers that a company has a reputation for treating its employees in an ill or disrespectful manner, he won't do business with it. On the other hand, if the company is known for treating its employees and customers alike with respect, he will bring it his business and refer others to its doorstep.

Spirituality in business for me means that you have enough life-boats on board in case of emergencies. It is much easier to design this into your company at the very foundation.

There are 100's of ideas that can make your operation unique in the marketplace. Always remember to ask yourself along the way as you are making decisions, "Is it spiritual?"… "Does it have meaning?"…and "Does it match up with my core values?"

Another company that I watched grow from one store to a huge success because of their principles was Costco. I have to confess that in the beginning, I was one individual who did not really give it much of a chance to succeed. What I did not know at the time was that they had designed success into their corporate culture from the beginning. Jeff Brotman, Chairman of Costco, was my attorney in 1974 when I opened The Breadline. He had gone through numerous ventures including a restaurant that I attempted to provide with some assistance. However, the restaurant was poorly designed from the beginning.

When Jeff Brotman and his partner designed Costco, success was designed into the very core of its foundation. To this day, I have never found anyone who has had one negative thing to say about working there. In fact, I've talked with many current and former Costco employees and they all say that it is a most wonderful environment in which to work. For me, this is the definition of a "spiritual place" to work. A place that honors the individual and and the well-being of their employees. This translates into an energy that is felt by customers as well.

Every time I shop at Costco, and it is often, I can feel the enthusiasm, the excitement and the energy of well-being throughout the store, and I honestly believe that this is one of the key ingredients responsible for the magnetism that Costco continues to experience. In my opinion, Jim Senegal, Costco CEO, is a genius of an architect in business design.

In the front of this book, I've printed one of my most favorite quotes, which comes from Frank Lloyd Wright, America's most famous architect. Speaking to a group of architectural students in 1950, he challenged them, "*As no stream can rise higher than its source, so you can give no more or better to architecture than you are. So why not go to work on yourself and make yourself in quality what you would have your buildings be.*"

And I would throw out the same challenge for every single businessperson. It is the same for your business. "*...So you can give no more to your business than you are. So go to work on yourself and make yourself in quality what you*

would have your business be." The idea of "spirituality" in our businesses is catching on more and more, but my guess is that it will be several years before it becomes the norm. We first have to give up the idea of power, position and control as the supreme goal, and rethink our definition of the bottom line. It is difficult to let go of the concept of competition vs. cooperation and collaboration.

Remember that we are connected on many levels, and business and our experience as entrepreneurs in the marketplace is a powerful way to feed this connection, which can have a positive influence in every other arena.

CHAPTER 22

ASKING FOR HELP

When is it appropriate to ask for help in your business? The short answer is "before you need it!"

Why is it that humans, especially men, don't want to ask for help? It is common knowledge that most males will refuse to ask for something as simple as directions.

Why do you think Moses led the Israelites through the desert for forty years? Was it because God was testing him… or maybe because he wanted them really to appreciate the Promised Land when they finally got there…or because Moses just refused to ask anybody for directions?

I will confess I fall into this final category. This behavior has at its core the belief that I am supposed to know what to do in every situation. In my own business, I am the one in charge, and it is not okay to let on that I don't have all the answers. I know that sometimes, and perhaps most of the time, the people working with me have the answers that I pretend to know.

Letting go of this ego-centered idea is a life-long process. It means I have to give up control and be vulnerable, which is a very scary idea for most of us. There is a simple way around this as is illustrated in the following story.

Tom came to the meeting yesterday all fired up with enthusiasm and a notebook filled with ideas. Tom is manager of a Texaco station with twelve auto mechanics all working on straight commission. A month ago, I asked all the employees of the company including all four service centers, how they would rate customer service on a scale of 1–100. I was being hired as a consultant to assist the owner in raising productivity for his entire company. Their answer was 80%. The managers decided that they wanted to have a goal in this area of 90%.

The general manager, Tom, and I had sat down one week before in a one-hour idea session for the purpose to raise service by 10%. We had only one rule: To make no judgment or decision on any idea for that hour. When we were finished, we had a whole page filled with a wide range of ideas. Tom was asked to give a ten-minute presentation at the next manager's meeting on the subject at hand. I simply reminded him, "You have your presentation right there from this meeting." The amazing thing was he did not use one idea that we came up with. Wisely, for the next thirty minutes, Tom shared from the ideas his people had offered when he sat down to ask for their help. The owner of the company was present and became so excited that I had to stop him twice just so we could continue the meeting.

What happened was simple and basic but most often forgotten in a business setting, and especially with men that know a lot about fixing cars! The owner had asked me for help. I asked Mark, the general manager, for help. We both asked Tom for help, and he in turn asked his mechanics for help. The end result was exciting, enthusiastic and rewarding to say the least.

Why is it that asking for help is so foreign to my nature? Perhaps I imagine if the world is going to work, I am the only one that can fix it. Maybe this comes from our age-old separatist view that we are not all working together to make this a better place to live.

When I ask for help, perhaps I am assisting in breaking down the barriers that separate us in the world, and for me, especially in the marketplace. It might follow that when I want to solve any problem, my first thought could be to ask for help, and then go to work on the problem. How I've always done it before has been to work myself into a hole, and then eventually ask for someone to help me get out.

The owner of this company with whom I worked was a very wise man. He asked for help before he needed it, and the end result was creating what he wanted.

I recall a quote from Kipling that I heard some years ago. I wrote it down at the time and have used this in several speeches since then. ***"What you do when you don't have to, determines what you will be when you can no longer help it."*** You might want to read this three or four times so it can really sink in.

Back in 1956, I enrolled in a Dale Carnegie course, and I can honestly say I am the only one I know that flunked this workshop. Of course, in reality, no one ever flunks, but here's what happened.

At the time, a fourteen-week course with twenty participants was not cheap. Every week, each of us gave a two-minute presentation and awards were given out to the three individuals who were the most improved and who gave the best presentations. In fourteen weeks, I never received even one prize, which usually was some fancy pen or pencil. This means there were a total of forty-two gifts awarded during the whole course and I did not receive even one of them…not even a pencil! Now you understand why I would say I "flunked."

Some years later, I joined Toastmasters, and over a five-year period of meeting every week, I did improve tremendously. Before taking the Dale Carnegie course, I would rather accept death over speaking in front of an audience of more than three people. So why am I telling you all this? I knew one day, sometime later in my life, I would be presenting in front of large audiences if I were going to fulfill my dreams.

I was actually asking for help long before I needed it! I even asked my minister at the time, Rev. Max Lafser, to give me private speaking lessons early on. He had never done something like this before, so we settled on a fee of $50.00/hour. For several years now, I have been speaking to a large number of churches as well as business conferences and Chambers of Commerce in various cities. I would consider myself a transformational speaker as opposed to a motivational speaker.

If I had not asked for help, and gone through the challenges of taking those classes, taking advantage of learning opportunities long before I needed them, I would not be the public speaker I am today.

Remember ~ "What you do when you don't have to, determines what you will be when you can no longer help it." ~ Rudyard Kipling

CHAPTER 23

LETTING GO OF CONTROL

I believe the most important aspect in growing a business is allowing others to take your place. In other words, in order for me to grow, for my business to grow, I will be most effective if I am consistently in the process of learning to let go of control, and looking for someone to take my place.

What does this mean?

In my own experiences, the most gut-wrenching, painful idea was to let someone else take over and manage my "baby," the business I had been working night and day with blood, sweat and tears to bring into a place of growth and maturity. The question at that moment is always, "*Do I want to expand and grow from here, or stay small and stay comfortable?*" The answer depends on the goals you've laid out for yourself and for your business.

In 1965, my partner, Joe Rutten, and I wrote down our goals for the new venture we were entering: To build and manage five or six Farrell's Ice Cream Parlour Restaurants in Washington State. At the time, we had no idea of exactly how we were going to do this since we each had only $2,000 to start with, our only assets at the time.

It took us a period of five years to create this initial investment. After operating our first store for over a year and demonstrating some success, it was time to think of opening a second location. When the opportunity presented itself with a landlord willing to build us a building on his property with a turnkey lease, we were faced with one of the toughest decisions of our lives. Who was going to manage our present store as well as the new store we were on the verge of building?

This was a very stretching, painful time as none of the first four managers we had hired were working out. We tried market managerial testings, multiple interviews, references and anything else we could think of that was coming down the pike. The average stay of any manager was three to four months. One manager we hired spent most of his time in the office, I believe, out of fear of the customers...or possibly the employees. Another manager had a gambling problem, and another had a sexual problem and was hitting on all our waitresses every chance he got. These are not items you find out about during the interview.

Now I knew instinctively that when you put someone in charge and give him or her the authority to hire and fire, you have to let go and trust that person. Yet, I remember one night sitting in my parked car looking into the restaurant to see whether the manager was doing everything right. It's tough to let go, but I made sure he didn't know I was watching from the parking lot.

I spent many nervous nights wondering what the manager was doing in my place. This time was a major period of letting go of control. It can be very costly as we figured each time we put a manager in place, it cost us at least $6,000. Managing forty to sixty people is not an easy task. Is learning to let go of control worth it? For us, if we had not gone through this, we never would have reached the goals we set out to accomplish.

Again, the vision determines what you will be willing to do to reach it. It would have been easier to lower our vision and just run one or two stores ourselves. But then we would not have learned one of life's greatest lessons, which is **Learning to Let Go of Control**. It is my opinion that being an entrepreneur and a business owner will teach you more about life than just about anything else you can do. Managing, hiring and training managers will teach you more about yourself and life's lessons than all the courses you might take at any university.

I have this theory and one that no institution of higher education will admit as they will lose customers if they did, and that is this: Take half the money you will spend on college and find the individuals doing the kind of work you wish to pursue. Offer to pay them this same amount to mentor you on all aspects of this profession, and I'll bet you, nine out of ten will take you up on this offer.

Of course, this will not work with licensed professions as the learning institutions and the state have long-standing agreements. However, for creative entrepreneurs, this idea will work wonders. I only wish I had done this instead of four years of engineering at college. To attend the school I attended now costs a minimum of $80,000 for four years, and that is if you're living at home! Just think of the valuable mentoring one could purchase for $40,000.

Talk about letting go of control! We have been told over and over again if you want to be a success, you need to earn a college degree. In this case, they are in control, not you. The ultimate of letting go would be for you to find someone to mentor you in the kind of work you find most fulfilling.

When I ask clients why they are not hiring and training someone to take their places, the answer is almost always, *"Well, I can't find anyone who can do this job as well as me!"* These are fear statements ~ **F**alse **E**vidence **A**ppearing **R**eal. In reality, I always had the choice to stay in fear or to keep trying until I found the right person to do the job.

One day, Neal hired me to work with his staff at his printing business. He had about twenty employees, and the first thing out of his mouth was, *"I just can't get any good help."* For me, this translated into, *"I can't find anyone I can trust."* Now the reality was that there was an abundance of good, hard-working people in his business. Because he was afraid to trust any of them, it became a self-fulfilling prophecy. They fulfilled his expectations. He was not about to let go of any control, and as a result, his business never grew beyond that point where he controlled everything himself.

The only way I was able to move forward was just to keep trying people until I found a good match. Why do so many business owners give up after only a few tries? Probably because it's easier to do it yourself than go through the problems and the agony of hiring and training someone to take your place. Believe me, it's worth it as it will give you the freedom to do more of the things you like to do. Just don't give up even after the second, third or fourth try.

Many years ago, I heard a well-known national consultant make this statement:

"When I go into a large company to work with the managers, I ask right up front who is training someone to take their place. I recommend the company let go of all the managers or supervisors that are not training their replacement."

This makes so much sense. If a business wants to grow, it can't afford to have any bottlenecks in the system. Anything that stops or slows down a growing system needs to move aside for it to flourish. This is true in nature and it is certainly true in a business setting. If you are not training someone to take your place, five or ten years from now, you will pretty much be in the same place you are now whether you own your own company or you are working in a company in a key position.

Letting go of control can happen on all levels of business. I have always made the most growth in my life when I have let go of control and trusted. Sure, fear sometimes creeps up, but you can move through that with enthusiasm for the task at hand.

Do you learn more when you are in control or when you are letting go of control?

If you know the answer to this question, then you are on your way to becoming a Creative Entrepreneur!

CHAPTER 24

THE BUSINESS OF "UNCERTAINTY"

"Uncertainty" ~ *The survival of your business depends on it.*

Bestselling author, Daniel H. Pink, states in his book, *A Whole New Mind: Moving From the Information Age to the Conceptual Age*:

"We are moving from an economy and society built on the logical, linear, computer-like capabilities of the information age to an economy and society built on the inventive, empathic, big-picture capabilities of what is rising in its place, the conceptual age."

There has never been a time of greater uncertainty in the world. And the business you are creating and growing is going to ride through waves of those awkward stages between the two trapezes.

I believe it is most important to be in touch with where we are in order to create the future we individually and collectively desire. Over twenty-five years ago, I had a vision of this shift occurring, but really did not know how or when it was going to take place. It will take many thousands of individuals like you and me to assist others in making this transition. For instance, I knew we would reach a time of critical mass when authenticity and integrity would become more supported, and duplicity would be exposed sooner. Just the fact that honesty and integrity in business will bring about tremendous change could not even be imagined some ten or twenty years ago.

Thank goodness we are finally here; a time when we can all put our right brain to good use, especially in the businesses we are creating and growing. And it is those very times of uncertainty in your business that are portals for golden opportunities of creativity.

For some fifty years now, I have been creating business ideas and concepts resulting in twenty business establishments integrating this right-brain approach with my engineering, linear perspective. In 1990, I decided to go on hiatus from leading seminars, giving speeches and consulting business owners for the simple reason that the business community was not yet ready for integrating this creative mode.

I intuitively knew things were going to change, eventually. The structures and systems that had worked in the past needed to fall apart so they could restructure into something different…more powerful. We are in a time when they are doing just that. Look around at all the systems that are in the process of failing; systems that no longer serve us. Religious institutions (where individual value/faith is sacrificed on behalf of religious systems driven by power and position), legal systems, the educational system, medical profession, and business.

For the entrepreneur, the structure of business and the marketplace is where we can have the greatest impact. Change and uncertainty are going to happen whether we like it or not. Our small planet is shifting and we have a choice to shift with it or fall off, so to speak.

We are definitely in an age of transformation with uncertainty around every corner. Changes in business will tend to occur more quickly than in other professions because we have large numbers of innovators and inventors in the business realm. These creative entrepreneurs do not have to wait for change. They are the change. You are the change! And because of this, it is truly a most exciting time in our history to be an entrepreneur.

I can recall a time in the 1950's and 60's when if you had a new product or service for a business project, it would often take years before you could potentially bring it to the marketplace. Not so today. Today we have accelerated that process where you can start a business in days, even hours and less.

Many of these changes are for the better. We are now given more time to experiment and fail, many times over even. Science has led the way in this. When working on a new discovery, scientists create a huge space for trial and error by calling their day-to-day failures hypotheses and experiments. They make it permissible to fail <u>repeatedly</u> until they come up with the result they want.

We need that same kind of tenacious spirit in business: to make it okay to fail many times over until we create the results we have envisioned. We are now at a place in history where we can speak openly about our mistakes. I compare this term to the process of film-making. When film directors are in the process of making movies, they have many "takes" until they get it right: "mis-takes."

I refer optimistically to some of the businesses I have created as "wind tunnels": those establishments devouring funds while producing little or no return on investment. Their value, however, was in serving as hypotheses in my on-going experiment to introduce a valued service or product, with integrity and quality, into the marketplace. Innovation in business is available to us as entrepreneurs more now than at any other time in our history. This age of transformation, this age of "uncertainty," is built for this kind of trial and error process. It is the very climate that will enable us to create a marketplace that will simultaneously bring profitable results while serving, with integrity our employees, customers and nurturing our planet…the triple bottom line.

The conceptual age we are now entering gives rise to a business model that is evolving at an accelerated rate. In a short while, we will no longer be able to use the term "business as usual." New terms are emerging on the marketplace horizon soon to become the norm, such as "business magic," "business transformation," and "conceptual age business."

These changes will require a whole new way of thinking and a whole new way of perceiving business. We are gradually moving into an era where we are integrating in the marketplace as the norm "right-brain" characteristics with predominantly left-brain, linear structures and systems. This transformative business with greater right/left brain integration will eventually become an art form much the same way as music, dance, photography, sculpture and painting are seen as art forms.

Each of us already possesses the ability to move into this transformation. It is a matter of putting what we already have to a greater good for humanity. Right now the marketplace provides us with abundant opportunities to practice and even master this new way of business.

In fact, even in this next week, in the guise of "uncertainty," there will be multiple opportunities for you to combine creative ways of thinking in transforming your business to the next level. Be on the look-out for them. I assure you, they will be around every corner!

CHAPTER 25

BUSINESS OF THE FUTURE

The old way of doing business is falling apart at the seams before our very eyes. This same "falling away" is occurring on a large scale in the core structures and systems that make up our institutional religion, politics, education, medicine and judiciary. The good news: When a system falls apart, it will always tend to reorder itself on a higher level.

We are in a time in history when we can look forward to a new and creative way of doing business. We are positioned as entrepreneurs to play a significant role in creating a new vision and implementing the ideas of this new paradigm.

Given the fact that a large number of entrepreneurs are finding themselves in this down economy, this true-life story is a timely one illustrating the above truth.

FALLING APART

It was April 1991 in Seattle. My wife, Jane, and I, along with incredible partners and managers, had built up our Yonny Yonson's healthy deli restaurant chain to six stores since 1977. Our largest store in the Columbia Center Building had been the first retail merchant there in 1984, and on our busy days, we were serving 700 customers per day our trademark chicken pot pies, cinnamon rolls, soups, sandwiches and yogurt.

Due to a series of breached agreements on the part of the former landlord, and the present management team of the new purchasing landlord, we were served with a ninety-day eviction notice, after seven years.

As a result of their actions, and refusal to allow us to sell our space to another restaurant owner, we ended up losing everything, the new restaurant, our home, our credit, and our credibility in the marketplace. Established restaurateurs in Seattle, my colleagues for some thirty-five years in the business, shook their heads in disbelief at the chain of events occurring. We did discover much later down the road that the individual who made the decision was eventually terminated from his job. In the interim, during that period, he would start each day by asking, "Let's see who can we get rid of in that building today." We weren't the only ones who were on the receiving end of his capricious ways.

We decided to forego investing any further energy into litigation, requiring large funding up front, and let it all fall apart. Being in financial survival mode at the time, Jane and I were walking through a field of landmines on a daily basis. Even the bank with which I had had a stellar relationship for more than twenty-five years turned its back.

After thirty-five years, my main identity as a successful restaurateur in the marketplace was falling apart.

Every day we would say to each other, "It can't get any worse," and every day it did. We were soon to be without a home, had nowhere to go, and many times, struggled to put food on the table for ourselves and our three-year old son.

The lowest point was on Valentine's Day, in 1992, when due to some vendor slipping through the cracks of the bankruptcy, the King County Sheriff knocked on our door and took away a used truck I had bought to paint houses so we could eat. Due to the generosity of my father-in-law, Amos, he paid the $1,000, and allowed me to get back the truck so I could paint some more houses.

Everything was falling away, and little by little, we began making a conscious choice just to let it all fall apart. We were learning that if you hang on tightly to whatever is organically falling away, that it will take a terrific toll. Once we moved into a place of allowing the falling-apart to occur, life actually became easier. We eventually were making choices to live in the moment, to support and trust each other, and for the next six years, our priority was showing up and living life fully, one moment at a time to the best of our abilities.

We did observe a bit of "karma" in action with the management company that evicted us. They no longer wanted a restaurant on the second floor, and ended up being unable to lease that space for seven years. When they finally leased the space, it was for only one-half of the monies asked of us. Interesting.

Out of that emptiness and huge falling away came all that we have created today. We would not have the marriage we have created these past twenty-seven years. We would not have rented part of our friends' home for more than a year, and would not have the friendship and memories with them.

We would not have purchased a piece of land and built the first strawbale home in King County, for $22,000, our only remaining asset.

I would not have written my first book, *Freedom From Work*. We would not have had all the 1000's of incredible memories of helping others to build GREEN, joining other pioneers in this field. Out of that falling apart came not one, but two successful painting companies, and another new book which you happen to be reading at the moment. The list is much longer than I can share here, but you get the idea.

And all that we learned about living in the moment, about letting fall apart what is already existing so it can reorder on a higher level, has also given us wisdom that can be applied to structures/systems in the marketplace and in any business.

With this fresh understanding, explore with me some of my vision for business in the future.

Here are some of my ideas of how future business will take shape:

1. Telling the truth with unconditional acceptance/ love.

We have now reached a point in our evolution where there is a new standard of transparency. In almost all business practices, there is a new demand that transparency exist from the top down, and duplicity be exposed. There also seems to be a critical mass emerging of awareness that we are all connected. This makes unconditional acceptance (love) a new priority.

2. Where every business owner is a visionary and is responsible for carrying the flame of that vision.

Each and every business will have a purpose and a mission that holds the focus of each individual working in that business. The business owner's primary purpose will be to create a space where all are contributing to the energy of that vision, and where he/she is responsible for conveying the life of that vision to the team.

3. Creating alignment with the vision/mission of all participants in the organization.

Alignment is when the energy of each individual is moving in support of the agreed-upon vision. Without alignment with a core vision, it is impossible to keep up with this more intense energy on the planet.

4. Creativity in Business.

There will be an accelerated use of our right brains in experimenting with unlimited ideas for advancement in every field. There are never too many ideas. Scientists call their activities hypotheses, experiments, theories. They program in their daily structure permission to fail repeatedly until in the end, they create the results approving/disproving their hypotheses. In the business realm, we will begin to do the same allowing the evolution of structures/systems to occur similar to those in the scientific realm. We will make it okay to experiment with our ideas while creating the business of the future.

5. Storytelling Required.

For a business to grow and evolve into something greater, it is essential to know the "stories" of the individuals with whom we are working. This will require the funding of retreats and seminars and other forms of networking to support this.

6. Systemic Thinking.

This is the macro vision ~ seeing the whole picture and how your business affects other organizations, the environment and all those with whom you come in contact.

7. Bringing FUN into your Business.

FUN at the work place will be the norm, and clocks, a thing of the past. Business owners will create through right-brain thinking games, structures, systems and methods all designed for workers to have FUN at their jobs. This will be an integral part of even the physical structure of the work place.

8. Spirituality in Business.

Your purpose in life and core values, including those of the spirit, will be an integral part of the place where you work.

9. Acknowledgement.

Acknowledgement of yourself and all other workers for their contributions to the mission. The number one thing people value most in life, and at work, is to be acknowledged, for the essence of their contributions to be seen and heard.

10. Strengths.

All business owners and workers will be using their strengths and talents to 100% capacity. Presently, in most companies, it is more like 20%.

11. Leadership.

We will continually be moving from "boss" (this is the way it's always been done) to "leaders" (I want your ideas on how we may innovate). Here are some specific characteristics defining the difference between a "boss" and a "leader."

1. A Boss tells what needs to be done.
   A Leader asks what needs to be done.

2. A Boss always has the answer.
   A Leader wants to know what <u>you</u> think.

3. A Boss is impatient.
   A Leader is willing to wait.

4. A Boss makes decisions with no reasons given.
   A Leader gives reasons for any decision.

5. A Boss cares primarily about him/herself.
   A Leader cares primarily for the workers.

6. A Boss will not do menial work.
   A Leader is willing to do any job needed to support the workers.

7. A Boss disregards boundaries.
   A Leader honors healthy boundaries.

8. A Boss cannot handle criticism.
   A Leader uses criticism constructively and improves.

9. A Boss always needs to be in control.
   A Leader is willing to give up control.

12. A Superior Learning Organization.

All company participants involved in their own personal growth ~ studying, going to classes and seminars. Having a coach, mentor or model to learn from and sharing what is learned.

Remember ~ "A learning organization is a place where people are continually discovering how they create their reality and how they can change it." ~ **Peter Senge**, *The Fifth Discipline*

CHAPTER 26

LIVING IN GRATITUDE

<u>Webster: Gratitude</u>: *"A feeling of thankful appreciation for favors or benefits received. Thankfulness. (See Grace)."*

When I first began setting goals for my personal and business life, I was doing it in a less powerful way. I was always setting my goals for some date in the future ~ "I want some day to accomplish this task or achieve this accomplishment." I would also assign specific dates when I was to realize certain goals. In the process, I was telling my subconscious that what I wanted was always sometime off in the distant future.

Many years later, I began learning that to create anything I wanted required that I picture it already in existence: What does it look like, feel like, smell like, and what would be my emotions if I had it in present time. Of course, time always enters into the equation, but it became much more powerful to practice the latter, and once I shifted, I began experiencing results immediately.

When my wife, Jane, and I were building our strawbale home in 2000–2002, everything seemed to take so long. After all, most homes are built in three or four months, but it took us approximately two years, primarily because we were doing the majority of it with cash. I look back on that period now and it doesn't feel as if the time were that long at all. The fun was in the journey, and the longer the journey, the more fun it was!

Halfway through the first year, I was getting anxious about this long journey, and Jane would remind me, "On some level, the house is already built…just be with that picture, and feel what that's like." Every time I wanted things to move much faster, she would just repeat this mantra. She was visualizing, and feeling the home already completed, and reminded me that according to quantum physics, the past, present and future were all in one moment anyway…so, in scientific terms, the home was already finished. This was an interesting concept I hadn't really considered, but it made sense.

We discovered as we practiced this, that the energy of this vision was orchestrating the details of this end result with greater ease and speed. Jane also reminded me to spend some time just feeling the gratitude of this beautiful home being completed, and the gratitude of our family and friends enjoying this nurturing place in the green hills of Washington. I began to move into this simple practice, and before long, the house was actually complete and we were living the reality of that vision. Gratitude begins long before the finish line, not after.

When I perceive that I don't have all I need to fulfill my commitments, I remind myself that what I have is enough, even if it is a very small amount. Giving thanks for what I have and being grateful appears to cause everything else to multiply! I challenge you to try this simple exercise, even if you don't believe in it at the moment. After all, you have nothing to lose.

Many years ago, when I gave my first speech at Toastmasters, I was so nervous during the week leading up to the talk that I couldn't concentrate on anything else. I decided to focus on the outcome I wanted, thereby taking my mind off the process of how I was going to perform. All week, I pictured in my mind's eye receiving the trophy for the best speech of the week. Guess what? It worked! To this day, all I remember is receiving the big prize, and I recall nothing about the actual talk.

I have used this concept of gratitude in creating businesses ever since and found that what it accomplishes, if nothing else, is that it causes what I am grateful for to happen much sooner than it did before I began doing the exercise.

Building a vision and being grateful not only for the outcome, but for exactly what is occurring in each moment, is now my daily exercise each morning and night. It takes only five or ten minutes and there is no reason ever to stop doing it. Being consciously grateful for all life holds in this moment and all that I will experience and create in the future is like a two-for-one. I even carry a "gratitude stone" in my pocket, just a simple stone that when I feel it during the day, it gives me a visceral reminder of all that is in my life deserving of deep gratitude.

This concept alone is definitely worth the $1,000 I mentioned at the beginning of the book. Just this one idea is of such value that if I had learned only one thing in the past fifty years, this would take the prize. Of course, I had to try it out many times before I believed it could work for <u>me</u>.

The whole of this book is a result of the gratitude I have been practicing in my life on a daily basis for all the rewarding and learning business experiences of my past, as well as those yet to come.

I am most grateful in this moment for the opportunity to share this with you, one more adventurous entrepreneur on the path of becoming more creative in each and every venture.

In accordance with recent discoveries of "Blue Zones," those zones on the planet where individuals are living long and healthy lives well into their 80's, 90's and even 100's, I am confident that in remembering these simple things, remembering that on some level, it has "already been built," enjoying the journey, treasuring every moment, and practicing gratitude daily along the way, you will experience a "blue zone" of sorts as a creative entrepreneur with a long and fulfilling life in your business ventures.

Wishing you all the best ~ Jack Fecker

About the Author

JACK FECKER's credibility originates from more than fifty years in the marketplace as a profitable entrepreneur, CEO, and business development consultant. His seminars, public speaking engagements, radio and TV appearances, have earned Jack the reputation as one of the most entertaining, humorous, wise and insightful speakers on the circuit today. Building more than twenty successful businesses, Jack is well known for his creation of one of Seattle's first major nightclubs, The Blue Banjo, where nineteen-year old Barbara Streisand stopped by and sang while standing on a chair during the Seattle World's Fair in 1962.

Perhaps the most popular of his business ventures was the Northwest territorial franchise (five stores) of Farrell's Ice Cream Parlours, with partner, Joe Rutten. The stores were the brainchild of Robert Farrell, with a total of 145 stores developed across the United States. Jack has counseled and spoken to thousands of professionals, and many of the most successful business owners have considered him their valued mentor. His first book, *Freedom From Work*, is a wealth of revealing stories and wisdom which have empowered many in bringing the best of who they are to all places of service, especially the workplace.

In this new book, *Becoming a Creative Entrepreneur*, Jack's focus is passing forward the wisdom gleaned from fifty years of rubber-meets-the-road experience as a business owner. Illustrating through numerous stories, humorous anecdotes and pragmatic action steps exactly how to integrate both left- and right-brain approaches, linear and creative, this is a book designed to support profitability at every stage of business. Married in 1984, Jack and his wife live in the green hills of Washington State. Jack continues creating and operating successful businesses while also enjoying life with his children and grandchildren.

SPEAKING ENGAGEMENTS/SEMINARS

Consulting/Mentoring/Media Interviews

Jack Fecker is available, nationally and internationally, for professional speaking engagements, seminars, consulting, media interviews and any event sponsored by individuals, associations, corporations and organizations supporting business professionals and the entrepreneurial spirit.

Jack is also available for individual/business/corporate mentoring.

==

FOR BOOKINGS AND AVAILABILITY

CONTACT: JANE BAKKEN

425.333.5246

HUNTRESS4AUTHORS@COMCAST.NET

WWW.BECOMINGACREATIVEENTRPRENEUR.COM

==

BOOK ORDERS:

WWW.BECOMINGACREATIVEENTRPRENEUR.COM